Paul Gayler

Great Homemade
SOUPS
A Cook's Collection

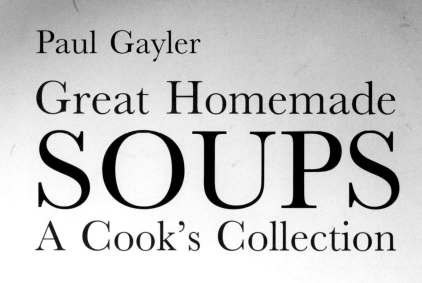

Paul Gayler

Great Homemade

SOUPS

A Cook's Collection

Photography by Lisa Linder

jacqui
small

*To my wife Anita and my family
for their continued love and support
with my endless hours of writing.*

First published in 2013 by
Jacqui Small LLP
An imprint of Aurum Press
74–77 White Lion Street
London N1 9PF
www.jaquismallpub.com

Text copyright © 2013 Paul Gayler

Publisher: Jacqui Small
Managing Editor: Lydia Halliday
Designer: Maggie Town
Editor: Hilary Mandleberg
Production: Peter Colley

ISBN: 978 19093 42231

A catalogue record for this book is
available from the British Library.

2015 2014 2013

10 9 8 7 6 5 4 3 2 1

Printed in China

contents

introduction

During my early training as a young chef, I was fortunate to work in all areas of the kitchen in some great hotels and restaurants. I can honestly say that the year I spent in the soup section ('the potage') was one of my most enjoyable cooking experiences. Huge pots filled with soups simmering gently on the heat were a delight to behold.

It was then that I learnt that making a great soup was truly an art. I discovered how to make all sorts of wonderful soups from smooth and creamy veloutés to hearty, more solidly nourishing soups involving vegetables, chunks of meat, fish, shellfish, and thick slices of bread. Later on I learnt about the more refined and subtle broths and consommés.

The chef used to tell me that a cook's reputation could rise or fall according to the quality of his or her soup – and how right he was. But don't let that deter you.

As you will see from the pages that follow, making fresh soup at home isn't rocket science. You will learn how to make the perfect stock base, just as I did, and then you can try your hand at any number of my recipes and variations, not to mention the garnishes that will give your soups the wow factor.

With soup now taking pride of place on the menus of the world's top restaurants, soups are making a real comeback. I urge you to join the trend, get out your pots and pans and discover the great soups of the world.

Happy cooking and happy eating!

Paul Gayler

> NOTE: All recipes in this book make 4 hearty servings or 6 smaller ones.

RIGHT: Pumpkin and Walnut Soup with Cèpes (recipe page 63)

about soups

the classification of soups

Soups are traditionally classified into two groups – clear soups and thick soups. These can then be further divided into different types.

clear soups

Clear soups are based on unthickened broth or stock. Broths and bouillons – which are obtained by simmering meats and/or vegetables – are the simplest type of clear soup.

Broth-style soups, garnished with a variety of meats, fish or vegetables, are more of a complete meal. They are especially popular in Asia, where they are flavoured with ingredients such as soy sauce or fish sauce.

Consommés are enriched broths that have been clarified (see pp.34–7) to make a soup that is crystal-clear. They are full of flavour and, with their sparkling clarity, are a delight to the eye. Served hot or cold, they make the perfect starter for an elegant dinner party.

thick soups

These soups are thickened either by adding a thickening agent – for example, rice or different types of grains and nuts – by adding a roux (see p.76) or by puréeing one or more of their ingredients.

Vegetable soups, made with a base of good stock, are naturally thickened, thanks to their starchy vegetable ingredients, for example they may contain potatoes or dried legumes.

The resulting soup can be puréed (though it is also possible to make a puréed soup from meat, fish or game) and you can then add milk or cream – though if you add cream, you end up with a cream soup. Whether you decide to add milk or cream, the soup should never be too thick – the consistency of single cream is about right.

Veloutés are puréed soups that have been enriched with a 'liaison' of cream and egg yolks, and sometimes a little butter.

bisques and chowders
Bisques are thickened soups made from shellfish, but today's chefs also make them from game such as hare and pheasant. All bisques are finished with cream.

Chowders are traditionally made with fish or shellfish and are finished with cream. In times gone by, chowders were thickened with bread.

chilled soups
These form another category of thick soups. Chilled soups are often served during the summer months. Their flavours can prove to be a revelation, especially when the soup is a fruit-based one.

fruit soups
Popular throughout Scandinavia, the Baltic and Eastern Europe, fruit soups are generally served cold but some can be served warm. In Asia, fruit-based soups often contain coconut milk and spices.

equipment

Soup-making requires very little in the way of equipment, apart from a good selection of knives in a variety of sizes, a few good-quality heavy-based saucepans, some chopping boards, wooden spoons, whisks, ladles and colanders, plus various bowls and a swivel peeler. In addition, it is worth having some equipment to help with blending your soup.

Of the various options, a blender is a great tool, especially if you are making creamy puréed soups (see pp.50–97) or soups in large quantities. Although blended soup is fairly smooth and silky, I still like to strain mine through a fine sieve after blending. That way I can obtain a really smooth, creamy-textured result.

A hand-held stick blender is another useful tool. It is ideal if you are making a small batch of puréed soup as you can blend the soup directly in the saucepan, thus minimising the washing-up. Handily, it can be rinsed clean quickly under hot water after use.

A food mill is a third option, but I find that it produces a soup that is neither lumpy nor totally smooth, so this is not my preferred choice.

garnishes and accompaniments

Many of the soups in this book include a garnish or accompaniment of some sort. There is sour cream to go with borscht, Gruyère-topped croûtons with French onion soup or aïoli for my simple fish soup.

However, there are many other simple, creative and interesting additions that can be used to elevate your soups. A soup such as minestrone has so much texture and visual character it doesn't need embellishing, but others, especially smooth, creamy soups, are sometimes pale in colour and don't have much going for them visually. Garnishing these to provide a contrasting flavour or texture can give them a real boost.

The techniques we chefs use can perhaps look a little pretentious but it isn't really that difficult to achieve the same effects at home. It may take you a little longer, but the finished results are well worth it, so here are my tips for making your soup out of this world.

herbs and flowers

Adding some freshly chopped or shredded herbs to a soup just before serving will really enliven it and add colour, especially to paler soups like potato or vichyssoise. Herbs to use include basil, parsley, coriander or chives. Even a simple sprig of herbs added on top can do the trick visually.

Herb-based sauces, such as pesto (see p.163) or salsa verde (see p.57), are delicious spooned onto soups, especially onto the chunkier and heartier ones. If you have used herbs in the preparation of the soup, ideally you should use a sauce made of the same herbs.

Or for a touch of something different, try topping your soup with a cluster of crispy deep-fried herbs. These can't fail to add some interesting texture.

Edible flowers also work well and nowadays you can buy many beautiful varieties, such as borage, pansies and dandelions. The flowers are sold individually or in mixed packs. When sprinkled onto the surface of a soup, the colours really catch the eye.

dairy-based garnishes

Smooth, puréed soups often need nothing more than a delicate swirl of cream, yoghurt, sour cream or crème fraîche to embellish them. Simply spoon your choice on top of the soup once it is in its serving bowl then, using a cocktail stick or the point of a small knife, gently swirl it around to form a delicate pattern on the surface.

Another option is a dollop of cream stiff enough to hold its shape. Whip it lightly until it is sufficiently thick then spoon it on. You can also stir some chopped herbs or delicate spices such as paprika or mild curry powder into the whipped cream, or you can simply sprinkle the herbs or spices on top. Either way, the cream will look attractive and taste delicious.

And if your fiery soup has turned out a bit too fiery, a simple dollop of cream on top can help calm things down.

Other dairy-based ideas include sprinkling freshly grated Parmesan cheese, Cheddar or Pecorino, or some crumbled blue cheese on the soup in the bowl.

bread-based garnishes

croûtons

Few soup garnishes are more appealing than a handful of homemade, buttery, fried croûtons (also known as sippets) to add a satisfying crunch.

You can buy packets of ready-made croûtons but the ones you make yourself will be streets better. Simply cut the crusts from some slices of medium white bread then cut the bread into evenly sized small cubes. Drizzle with a little extra virgin olive oil and bake in a medium oven for 6–8 minutes until golden and crispy or – and to my mind these taste even better – fry in a little butter. Your croûtons will keep in a sealed container for 2–3 days.

If you are feeling more adventurous, you could try frying the croûtons in a little garlic butter, add some freshly chopped herbs to the butter as the croûtons fry or sprinkle the croûtons with grated Parmesan cheese just before you remove them from the pan.

bruschettas, crostini and tartines

Bruschettas are made using slices of open-textured, usually Italian, bread, such as ciabatta. They are an excellent way of using up bread that is a day or two old. Toast it on both sides and while it is still warm, rub with garlic and drizzle with extra virgin olive oil.

You can also use your bruschettas as a base for a variety of toppings, such as salsas, chopped tomatoes or roasted Mediterranean vegetables. Garnished with delicate basil leaves, they look and taste great. Other toppings include cured meats, crispy bacon and poached or flaked smoked fish, such as salmon or smoked haddock – the list goes on.

In France, tartines, made from a baguette, are similar, then there are also the Italian crostini. Traditionally, crostini and tartines are thinner than bruschettas and are usually topped with savoury sauces and spreads such as tapenade or pesto (see p.163), or even with sliced or crumbled cheese.

However, there is no need to limit yourself to the traditional loaf of bread if you want tasty, crunchy soup toppings. Try the following:

- **Left-over pitta bread**, drizzled with extra virgin olive oil and dusted with za'atar, a Middle-Eastern spice mix made of thyme, sesame seeds and savory. Then bake at 160°C (325°F/Gas 3) for 5 minutes, or until crisp and golden.
- **Baked cubes of naan bread**, dusted with chilli powder or other Indian spices.
- **Shredded corn tortilla strips**, deep-fried until crispy – great for Mexican-inspired soups.
- **Mini poppadums**, broken into pieces for adding some crunch and extra flavour to dhal or Mulligatawny soup.
- **Freshly popped popcorn** dusted with spices as a great addition to a sweetcorn-based or chowder-style soup.

toasties

Toasties are small toasted sandwiches that can be filled with all manner of ingredients. Be creative and make a filling to complement your soup. Sliced cured meats, grated or sliced cheese and chopped sautéed mushrooms are just a few possibilities. You can make your toasties in advance and simply toast them under a grill when needed or cook them by frying in butter. Then just cut into small squares to serve.

RIGHT, from top: Croûtons, Gougères, Olive Tapenade Straws

baked cheese garnishes

cheese straws (makes 12)

350g (12oz) ready-rolled puff pastry (thawed if frozen)
a little flour, for dusting
75g (2½oz/⅔ cup) finely grated Parmesan or mature Cheddar cheese

Unroll the pastry on a lightly floured surface, scatter with half the cheese, then fold the pastry in half. Roll out to a thickness of 1.5cm (⅝in), then cut into 1cm (½in) strips, 10cm (4in) long. Holding the ends of each strip, twist in opposite directions to form a spiral. Arrange, slightly apart from each other, on a baking tray lined with greaseproof paper. Scatter with the remaining cheese and bake in a preheated oven at 200°C (400°F/Gas 6) for 10–12 minutes, or until golden. Remove and cool on a wire rack. Serve immediately or store in a sealed container in a dry place for 2–3 days.

Try these variations:
For olive tapenade straws, spread the pastry with 75g (2½oz) olive tapenade (see p.78) before folding it in half.
For sunblush tomato straws, spread the pastry with a coarse purée of sunblush tomatoes before folding it in half.
For herb straws, sprinkle mixed chopped herbs over the pastry before folding it in half.

cheese scones (makes 20–25)

These light, fluffy cheese scones are a delicious complement both to creamy soups, such as potato or celeriac soup, and to hearty, chunky soups, like farmhouse or lentil soup. As a variation, try adding 75g (2½oz) chopped fried bacon or chopped fried cooking chorizo to the recipe, or some chopped herbs.

225g (8oz/1⅔ cups) self-raising flour, plus extra for dusting
½ tsp sea salt
1 tsp baking powder
75g (2½oz/⅔ cup) mature Cheddar or Parmesan cheese, finely grated
50g (1¾oz/3½ tbsp) unsalted butter
150ml (5fl oz/⅔ cup) buttermilk or whole milk
1 beaten egg, to glaze

Sift the flour, salt and baking powder together into a bowl. Add 50g (1¾oz/½ cup) of the cheese then rub in the butter until thoroughly mixed. Add the buttermilk or milk and mix together gently to form a soft dough. Turn out onto a lightly floured work surface and knead gently. Do not overwork the dough or the scones will be tough and heavy. Roll out the dough to about 2cm (¾in) thick then cut into 5cm (2in) rounds using a plain biscuit cutter. Place the scones, slightly apart from each other, on a baking tray lined with greaseproof paper. Brush liberally with the beaten egg then sprinkle with the remaining cheese. Bake in a preheated oven at 220°C (425°F/Gas 7) for 10–12 minutes, or until cooked and golden. Transfer to a wire rack to cool slightly before serving.

herby cheese sablés (makes 40)

125g (4½oz/1 cup) plain flour, plus extra for dusting
75g (2½oz/⅓ cup) unsalted butter
125g (4½oz/1 cup) mature Cheddar, Gruyère or Parmesan cheese, finely grated
1 small egg, lightly beaten
1 tsp finely chopped rosemary leaves
pinch of mustard powder
sea salt and freshly ground black pepper

Put all the ingredients in a bowl and mix together gently to form a soft, paste-like dough. Turn out onto a lightly floured surface and knead gently. Wrap in clingfilm and refrigerate for 1 hour. Remove from the fridge and roll the dough out to about 5mm (¼in) thick, then cut into 5cm (2in) rounds using a plain biscuit cutter. Knead the trimmings together, re-roll and cut out more rounds. Put the rounds on a baking tray lined with greaseproof paper and bake in a preheated oven at 200°C (400°F/Gas 6) for 10 minutes, or until golden and crisp. Remove and cool on a wire rack. Serve immediately or store in a sealed container in a dry place for 2–3 days.

gougères (makes 30)

These little cheese puffs are wonderful and can be made with all manner of tasty fillings. My favourites are creamy herb-cheese mixtures. The gougères can be made in advance and kept in a sealed container for 2–3 days.

75g (2½oz/⅓ cup) unsalted butter
pinch of sea salt
100g (3½oz/¾ cup) plain flour, sieved
3 eggs
100g (3½oz/1 cup) Gruyère or Emmenthal cheese, coarsely grated
a little beaten egg to glaze

Melt the butter in a pan with 200ml (7fl oz/¾ cup) water and a good pinch of salt, then bring to the boil. Remove from the heat and rain in the flour a little at a time, beating vigorously with a wooden spoon until the mixture is glossy and smooth, pulls away from the sides of the pan, and forms a ball. Beat for 1 minute more over the lowest heat. Let the mixture cool slightly before beating in the eggs, one at a time. Ensure each egg is thoroughly beaten in before adding another. Beat in 75g (2½oz/⅔ cup) of the cheese. Put the dough in a piping bag fitted with a 1cm (½in) plain tube then pipe into small mounds on a baking tray lined with greaseproof paper. Brush each mound with a little beaten egg wash then sprinkle over the remaining cheese. Bake in a preheated oven at 190°C (375°F/Gas 5) for 30–35 minutes, or until cooked and golden. Cool on a wire rack before filling each gougère with your favourite filling or before storing in a sealed container in a dry place for 2–3 days.

OPPOSITE, clockwise from top right: Shredded Corn Tortilla Strips, Za'atar Pitta Crisps, Cheese Scones, a selection of Bruschettas and Crostini, Crispy Deep-fried Herbs, Herby Cheese Sablés, Toasties

a miscellany of soup toppings

nuts and seeds

Nuts and seeds add a delightful textural element to a soup. Try roasted nuts, such as almonds, hazelnuts, pine nuts or cashews, or seeds, such as sunflower or pumpkin.

crispy-fried garnishes

Try the following:
- **Crispy-fried slices of root vegetables,** such as pumpkin, celeriac and parsnip.
- **Crispy-fried shallots** make a delicious addition to some Asian soups.
- **Crispy-fried shellfish or seafood** in a crispy tempura-style batter are great for adding texture and flavour.

salsas and relishes

A spoonful of salsa, freshly made from tomatoes, basil and peppers, or a chutney-style relish can all add flavour and wake up soups such as avocado soup or chilled cucumber soup. The salsa can be placed directly on the surface of the soup or on top of sautéed croûtons.

flavoured oils

Flavoured oils add a nice contrast to a soup. Simply drizzle some over the surface.

Try the following:
- **For garlic oil,** heat 1 tsp crushed garlic in 120ml (4fl oz/½ cup) extra virgin olive oil over a low heat for 5 minutes.
- **For herb oil,** purée in a blender a handful of your favourite herb or herbs with 100ml (3½fl oz/scant ½ cup) extra virgin olive oil.
- **For spiced oil,** infuse 1 tsp spice (paprika, cumin, etc.) in 100ml (3½fl oz/scant ½ cup) extra virgin olive oil.
- **For citrus oil,** infuse 2 tsp grated orange, lemon or lime zest in 100ml (3½fl oz/scant ½ cup) extra virgin olive oil.

After infusing the oil, for the best flavour, leave for 2 days in a sealed jar then strain though a fine muslin or sieve before using.

citrus zest

Citrus fruits add a lovely tang. Use a zester to make fine shreds of citrus fruits like lemon, orange and lime, or use a fine grater to obtain a finely grated zest.

dried citrus powders

I also love to prepare dried fruit powders from citrus fruits. These are simply wonderful sprinkled delicately onto soups, whether hot or chilled. You can also add them to cream before stirring into a soup. And as well as using them to garnish your soup, they are great added to fish or chicken before grilling, or sprinkled over a salad such as a salmon or smoked meat salad.

Fruit powders are simple to make. Peel off ribbons of zest using a swivel peeler. Put the zest on a baking tray lined with greaseproof paper, then put in a low oven at 50°C (120°F) overnight to dry. Remove and cool before grinding to a fine powder in a spice or coffee grinder. The powder will keep well for a few months in a sealed container or in a jar in the fridge.

flavourful homemade stocks

The basis of a great homemade soup is a great homemade stock. I know that for many home cooks the convenience of the bouillon cube is sometimes just too alluring to be ignored and I would be lying if I said I hadn't ever used the odd one myself on occasion. Luckily we now have a pretty good range of ready-made chilled stocks in the supermarkets and these should be your first port of call if you really, really don't have time to make your own.

But while there is no denying that making stock at home can be time-consuming, the extra effort undoubtedly yields great rewards flavour-wise. I suggest you try to make your own in bulk and keep it in small amounts in your freezer, ready to use when needed. That gives you the best of both worlds – great taste and convenience.

Don't forget to allow plenty of time – about 3–4 hours – for frozen stock to defrost completely at room temperature. Alternatively, remove from the freezer the day before needed and defrost it slowly overnight in the fridge.

Making a great stock is not difficult. Meat or fish stocks are made by slowly simmering the bones and trimmings of meat or fish with vegetables and aromatic seasonings. Fish stock is cooked for a shorter period than meat stock, which keeps the stock clean and fresh-tasting. Only fresh vegetables and seasonings are used in the preparation of vegetable stocks, which makes them far more delicate. They are also cooked for a lot less time than meat stocks, and so retain the light flavours of the vegetables themselves.

Whichever type of stock you are making, there is one rule you need to follow to ensure success every time. Never ever treat the stock pot as a rubbish bin. The quality of the ingredients you put in will determine the quality of the stock you get out. Too often cooks view stock-making as an opportunity to use up past-their-best odds and ends from the fridge or from the kitchen vegetable rack. This is wrong. Good-quality fresh ingredients should be the order of the day at all times. Remember rubbish in – rubbish out!

white chicken stock

2kg (4½lb) raw chicken carcasses or a mixture of chicken legs and wings

5 litres (8 pints/4.4 quarts) cold water

2 onions, coarsely chopped

2 celery sticks, coarsely chopped

2 large carrots, coarsely chopped

1 leek, trimmed and coarsely chopped

1 tsp black peppercorns

1 bayleaf

1 bouquet garni

makes 3 litres/5¼ pints/2.6 quarts

Put the chicken in a large saucepan, add the cold water to cover and slowly bring to the boil. Skim occasionally to remove any impurities that float to the surface.

Add the remaining ingredients, reduce the heat and simmer gently for 4 hours.

Remove from the heat and strain through a fine sieve. Leave to cool then refrigerate until required.

Variation: Asian Chicken Stock Proceed as for the basic stock but add a 2.5cm (1in) piece of sliced root ginger, 2 sliced garlic cloves and a small handful of coriander stalks.

how to make the perfect
brown chicken stock

3 tbsp sunflower oil

2kg (4½lb) raw chicken carcasses or a
mixture of chicken legs and wings

2 onions, coarsely chopped

2 celery sticks, coarsely chopped

2 large carrots, coarsely chopped

1 leek, trimmed and coarsely chopped

2 sprigs of thyme

50g (1¾oz/⅓ cup) tomato purée

5 litres (8 pints/4.4 quarts) cold water

1 bouquet garni

1 tsp black peppercorns

1 bayleaf

makes 3 litres/5¼ pints/2.6 quarts

1 Preheat the oven to 220°C (425°F/Gas 7).

2 Heat half the oil in a large roasting tin in the preheated oven, then add the chicken carcasses and roast, uncovered, for 40 minutes, or until browned.

3 Meanwhile, heat the remaining oil in a large frying pan. When it is hot, add the prepared vegetables, thyme and tomato purée. Fry until brown and lightly caramelised.

4 Put the browned bones and vegetables in a large saucepan, add the cold water to cover and slowly bring to the boil. Skim occasionally to remove any impurities that float to the surface (see picture overleaf).

5 Add the bouquet garni, peppercorns and bayleaf, reduce the heat and simmer gently for 4 hours.

6 Remove from the heat and strain through a fine sieve. Leave to cool, then refrigerate until needed (see picture overleaf).

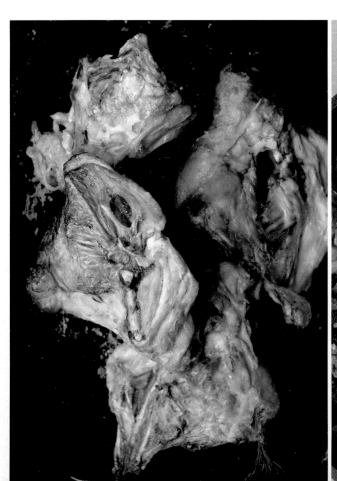

2

3

4

6

beef or game stock

3 tbsp sunflower oil

2kg (4½lb) beef or veal bones, or game bones if making Game Stock

400g (14oz) beef trimmings or game trimmings if making Game Stock

2 onions, coarsely chopped

2 celery sticks, coarsely chopped

2 large carrots, coarsely chopped

2 sprigs of thyme

50g (1¾oz/⅓ cup) tomato purée

5 litres (8 pints/4.4 quarts) cold water

1 bouquet garni

1 tsp black peppercorns

1 bayleaf

makes 3 litres/5¼ pints/2.6 quarts

Preheat the oven to 220°C (425°F/Gas 7).

Heat half the oil in a large roasting tin in the preheated oven. When it is hot, add the bones and beef trimmings and roast, uncovered, for 1 hour, or until browned, stirring occasionally so they do not burn.

Meanwhile, heat the remaining oil in a large frying pan, then add the prepared vegetables, thyme and tomato purée. Fry until brown and lightly caramelised.

Put the browned bones and vegetables in a large saucepan, add the cold water to cover and slowly bring to the boil. Skim occasionally to remove any impurities that float to the surface.

Add the bouquet garni, peppercorns and bayleaf, reduce the heat and simmer gently for 4 hours.

Remove from the heat and strain through a fine sieve. Leave to cool then refrigerate until required.

Variation: Lamb or Pork stock Proceed as for the basic Beef or Game Stock but replace the beef, veal or game bones and the beef trimmings with the same weight of meaty lamb bones or pork bones.

vegetable stock

1 onion, coarsely chopped

1 leek, trimmed and coarsely chopped

75g (2½oz) celeriac, peeled and coarsely chopped

2 large carrots, coarsely chopped

1 celery stick, coarsely chopped

2 garlic cloves, chopped

2 sprigs of thyme

1 bayleaf

1 tsp black peppercorns

3 litres (5¼ pints/2.6 quarts) cold water

makes 2 litres/3½ pints/1.8 quarts

Put all the ingredients in a large saucepan and bring to the boil. Skim occasionally to remove any impurities that float to the surface.

Reduce the heat and simmer gently for 1 hour. Do not overcook or the vegetables will lose their fresh flavour.

Remove from the heat and strain through a fine sieve. Leave to cool then refrigerate until required.

how to make the perfect
fish stock

25g (scant 1oz/2 tbsp) unsalted butter

1 leek, trimmed and
coarsely chopped

1 onion, coarsely chopped

1.5kg (3lb 3oz) fish bones (preferably from
white fish), chopped into
small pieces

juice of ¼ lemon

2 litres (3½ pints/1.8 quarts)
cold water

1 bayleaf

½ tsp black peppercorns

6 coriander seeds

makes 1.5 litres/2¾ pints/1.3 quarts

1 Heat the butter in a pan then add the leek and onion and cover with a lid. Cook over a low heat for 5 minutes until softened. Add the fish bones, squeeze over the lemon juice, cover again and cook for 5 minutes more.

2 Pour the water over and add the bayleaf, peppercorns and coriander seeds. Bring to the boil.

3 Reduce the heat and simmer gently for 20 minutes. Skim occasionally to remove any impurities that float to the surface.

4 Remove from the heat and strain through a fine sieve. Leave to cool then refrigerate in a sealed container until required. If not using within 2–3 days, divide into 600ml (1 pint/2½ cups) batches and freeze. The stock will keep for up to 3 months in the freezer.

Variation: Asian fish stock Proceed as for the basic stock but add 1 sliced garlic clove, 2 stalks of lemongrass, tough outer layers removed and the rest coarsely chopped, 2.5cm (1in) piece of root ginger, sliced, 1 tbsp fish sauce (nam pla) and 2 tbsp Chinese rice wine or dry sherry.

natural broths and consommés

Of all the wild mushrooms that you can forage for in the autumn months, porcini (cèpes) are, in my opinion, the most flavourful. They do wonders for a simple broth like this one. I find I get an even more delicious flavour if I use a combination of fresh and dried porcini. The eggs are cooked very slowly, which retains their brilliant yellow colour and creamy interior. Although they take a while to cook, it is worth the effort as they taste delicious dunked in the rich wild mushroom broth.

porcini broth
with dropped confit eggs and herbs

500ml (17fl oz/2 cups) sunflower oil

4 large egg yolks

25g (scant 1oz/½ cup) dried porcini (cèpes)

200ml (7fl oz/¾ cup) hot water

2 tbsp extra virgin olive oil

1 small onion, finely chopped

1 garlic clove, crushed

2 tbsp coarsely chopped herbs (such as rosemary, chives or chervil)

75ml (2½fl oz/⅓ cup) dry white wine

60ml (2fl oz/¼ cup) Madeira or dry sherry

750ml (1¼ pints/3 cups) brown chicken stock (see p.19)

400g (14oz/6 cups) fresh porcini, wiped clean and thinly sliced

sea salt and freshly ground black pepper

20g (¾oz) mixed small herbs (such as tarragon, chives or chervil), to garnish

Firstly start cooking the eggs. Preheat the oven to 50°C (120°F). Pour the sunflower oil in a shallow roasting tin and carefully immerse the egg yolks in the oil, ensuring they are covered. Place in the preheated oven and cook for 1 hour.

Meanwhile, prepare the soup. Rehydrate the dried porcini by putting them in a large bowl, adding the hot water and leaving to soak for 30 minutes.

Heat the olive oil in a large pan then add the onion, garlic and herbs. Reduce the heat and cook for 10 minutes until softened.

Add the wine, cook for 2 minutes, then add the Madeira or sherry, stock and the soaked porcini and their liquid. Simmer very gently over a low-medium heat for 20 minutes.

Meanwhile, line a sieve with a double-thickness piece of damp muslin or with a large, strong coffee-filter paper. Strain the broth through this into a clean pan.

Add the fresh porcini to the broth, bring to the boil, then reduce the heat and simmer gently for 2 minutes. Season with salt and pepper.

Divide the hot broth between 4 individual soup bowls. Remove the egg yolks from the oven and carefully lower one into each bowl of broth. Garnish with herbs and serve immediately.

Variation: Porcini and Truffle Broth Proceed as for the basic soup but for an extra treat, when you add the fresh porcini, also add 100ml (3½fl oz/½ cup) canned truffle juice and a few slices of truffle if your budget allows it.

THIS PAGE AND OPPOSITE: My Simple
Fish Soup with Aïoli (recipe page 32)

It is fair to say there are as many versions of fish soup as there are cooks. This simple recipe makes a wonderful lunch or light supper dish. The fish is steamed in the flavoured stock and then served in the soup. The addition of the toasted baguette slices and garlic mayonnaise make it a hearty, rather substantial meal. If you want to make the soup more impressive, simply add some cleaned scallops or prawns with the fish. You can use just about any fish for this soup but make sure that it is firm-fleshed and always extremely fresh.

my simple fish soup with aïoli

2 small onions, thinly sliced

300g (10oz) small waxy potatoes, peeled and thinly sliced

2 carrots, thinly sliced

1 x 200g (7oz) canned chopped tomatoes

12 red cherry tomatoes

4 baby fennel, trimmed

1 celery stick, thinly sliced

3 tbsp torn flat-leaf parsley

pinch of fresh or dried saffron

750ml (1¼ pints/3 cups) fish stock (see p.24) or water

1.5kg (3lb 3oz) fish (such as monkfish, mullet, bream or any other firm-fleshed fish), cut into 5cm (2in) pieces

juice of ¼ lemon

sea salt and freshly ground black pepper

To serve

1 small baguette, thinly sliced and toasted

100ml (3½fl oz/scant ½ cup) garlic mayonnaise

Put all the ingredients except the fish, fish stock and the lemon juice in a heavy-based shallow pan. Cover with the fish stock or water and bring to the boil. Reduce the heat and simmer for 20 minutes, or until the vegetables are just cooked.

Carefully put the fish on top of the vegetables, cover with a lid and steam the fish gently for 5 minutes, or until cooked.

Remove the fish and vegetables with a slotted spoon and divide between 4 large soup plates or bowls.

Add the lemon juice to the cooking broth and season to taste, then pour the broth over the fish. Serve with the toasted baguette slices and the garlic mayonnaise.

Ajiaco is a potato broth-style soup from Bogotá in Colombia. It features two types of potato – floury and waxy – and is enriched with sour cream. It is finished with *aji*, a condiment made from blending chopped onion, garlic and coriander.

ajiaco

1.5 litres (2¾ pints/1.3 quarts) white chicken stock (see p.17), plus extra if required

2 large chicken breasts, skin removed

1 bayleaf

400g (14oz) floury potatoes, peeled and cut into 1cm (½in) cubes

300g (10oz) small new potatoes, peeled and cut in half

200g (7oz/1¼ cups) sweetcorn kernels (fresh, frozen or canned)

½ tsp finely chopped green chilli

3 tbsp baby capers, rinsed and drained

100ml (3½fl oz/scant ½ cup) sour cream

2 small firm but ripe avocados, cut into 1cm (½in) cubes

sea salt and freshly ground black pepper

wedges of lime, to garnish (optional)

For the aji

1 onion, finely chopped

½ garlic clove, crushed

4 tbsp coarsely chopped coriander

Bring the stock to the boil in a large pan, add the chicken breasts and bayleaf, bring back to the boil, then reduce the heat and simmer for 12–15 minutes, or until the chicken breasts are tender. Skim off any impurities that float to the surface. Remove the breasts with a slotted spoon and when cool, cut into shreds. Set aside.

Meanwhile, add the floury potatoes to the pan and cook gently for 25 minutes, or until tender. Remove the bayleaf, then stir to break down the potatoes into the broth. Add the new potatoes and a little more stock if necessary to cover. Cook until the potatoes are just tender.

Meanwhile, make the *aji* by putting the onion, garlic and coriander in a small blender. Blitz to a coarse purée and set aside.

Add the sweetcorn kernels, chilli, capers and cream to the soup pan. Cook for 10 minutes more. Add the avocado, return the chicken to the pan and season to taste.

Divide between 4 individual soup bowls, sprinkle over some of the *aji* and serve immediately, garnished with the lime, if used.

how to make the perfect
chicken consommé

Consommé is thought by many to be the true test of a good cook. When made correctly, it will be crystal clear and full of flavour, and it should be a rich light-gold colour, bordering on amber. Making consommé may be a little more time-consuming than making many other soups, but it is worth the effort. To yield the best results, start with a well-flavoured stock. The clarification process isn't really that difficult if you are patient and follow my instructions. Consommés can be made from beef, game, shellfish and even vegetables and they can be served either hot or cold.

500g (1lb 2oz) chicken breast, skin removed and finely minced

3 egg whites

I carrot, finely minced

1 onion, finely minced

1 leek, white part only, finely minced

1 celery stick, finely minced

few leaves of flat-leaf parsley, finely minced

few leaves of fresh tarragon, finely minced

4 white peppercorns

1 tsp sea salt

1 litre (1¾ pints/4 cups) cold brown chicken stock (see p.19)

1 Put the chicken, egg whites, carrot, onion, leek, celery, parsley, tarragon, peppercorns, salt and 250ml (9fl oz/1 cup) of the stock in a large heavy-bottomed pan. Blend together well with a wooden spoon or clean hands until thoroughly mixed together.

2 Add the remaining chicken stock and mix again. Boil rapidly for 10 seconds, give a final stir, reduce the heat, then simmer very gently for 25–30 minutes without stirring.

3 As the stock continues to simmer, it will start to appear a little cloudy and a crust will eventually form on the surface.

4 Meanwhile, line a sieve with a double thickness of damp muslin or a large, strong coffee-filter paper. Carefully pierce through the crust on the surface of the consommé and ladle the consommé into the lined sieve, without disturbing the crust.

5 Once strained, the consommé should be perfectly clear. If any fat droplets remain, remove them with a small ladle or piece of damp kitchen paper drawn across the surface. Discard the crust.

6 Transfer the clarified consommé to a clean pan and reheat gently. Divide between 4 individual soups bowls and serve immediately.

4

5

Variations: Chicken, Lemongrass and Ginger

Consommé Proceed as for the basic soup but add 2 stalks of lemongrass, tough outer layers removed and the rest coarsely chopped, and a 2.5cm (1in) piece of grated root ginger to the minced chicken and egg whites, then proceed as for the Chicken Consommé. Add 2 tbsp coarsely chopped coriander just before serving.

Herb Consommé Proceed as for the basic soup. Add a good handful of coarsely chopped fresh mixed herbs, such as tarragon, flat-leaf parsley or chervil, to the minced chicken and egg whites. When reheating the consommé, add 50g (1¾oz) herbs, leaving them to infuse for 2–3 minutes before serving.

Jewish Matzo Ball Soup Matzo ball soup is the pride of Jewish cooking. Basically, it is chicken consommé with tiny matzo-meal dumplings, vegetables and parsley.

To make the matzo balls, mix together in a bowl 3 eggs, 3 tbsp water, 45g (1½oz/3 tbsp) unsalted butter, 1 finely chopped onion and 75g (2½oz/⅓ cup) matzo meal. Season to taste.

Refrigerate for 1 hour then roll into 2cm (¾in) balls using wet hands. Add to 1 litre (1¾ pints/4 cups) chicken consommé together with 75g (2½oz/½ cup) each of cubed carrots and celery. Bring to the boil then reduce the heat and simmer for about 40 minutes, or until the balls are firm. Just before serving, add some coarsely chopped parsley.

beef or game consommé

A beef or game consommé is made in roughly the same way as Chicken Consommé. Proceed as for the basic soup but replace the brown chicken stock with the same quantity of beef or game stock and the chicken meat with the same weight of minced beef or game. Before serving, stir in 100ml (3½fl oz/scant ½ cup) Madeira or dry sherry.

Variation: Beef Consommé with Watercress and

Lemon Dumplings For the dumplings, mix together in a bowl 50g (1¾oz/1 cup) breadcrumbs, ¼ tsp grated lemon zest, 1 tbsp lemon thyme leaves or 1 tbsp thyme leaves, 25g (scant 1 oz/2 tbsp) softened, unsalted butter and 1 egg yolk. Roll the mixture into small marble-sized balls and refrigerate for 30 minutes. Add to boiling water, reduce the heat and poach for 15 minutes, or until the dumplings bob to the surface. Drain and set aside until ready to use.

Prepare 1 litre (1¾ pints/4 cups) beef consommé. Before serving, add the dumplings and 50g (1¾oz) small watercress leaves.

THIS PAGE: Egg-flower Soup
(recipe page 41)

OPPOSITE: Peking Duck Broth
with Wontons and Green Onions
(recipe page 40)

This is great way to use Chinese barbecue duck; the leg meat provides the wonton filling, the breasts are added to the soup, while the carcass is the base for a great-tasting broth. I often add some Asian mushrooms, such as shiitake or shimeji mushrooms. Homemade barbecue duck can be delicious and rewarding but alas, it is also time-consuming. I recommend you buy your duck ready-cooked from an Asian supermarket.

peking duck broth with wontons and green onions

1 Chinese barbecue duck

For the wontons

1 tbsp coarsely chopped coriander

2 spring onions, coarsely chopped

1 tbsp oyster sauce

2cm (¾in) piece of root ginger, finely chopped

12 Chinese wonton wrappers

1 egg, lightly beaten, for the egg wash

For the broth

1 litre (1¾ pints/4 cups) Asian chicken stock (see p.17) or white chicken stock (see p.17)

2.5cm (1in) piece of root ginger, thinly sliced

2 star anise

2 tbsp soy sauce

2 tbsp hoisin sauce

2 tbsp oyster sauce

4 spring onions, shredded

1 garlic clove, crushed

2 carrots, thinly sliced

1 x 125g (4½oz) canned sliced bamboo shoots, rinsed and drained

Remove all the meat from the duck and set the carcass aside. Cut the breasts into slices about 1cm (½in) thick and set aside. Chop the leg meat into small cubes and put in a bowl.

To make the wontons, add the coriander, spring onions, oyster sauce and ginger to the leg meat and mix together well. The mixture should be fairly thick and not too wet.

Lay out the wonton wrappers on a flat surface. Using a teaspoon, put mounds of the mixture in the centre of each sheet. Brush the edges of each with a little egg wash, then gather the edges together at the top, pinch and twist to seal. Refrigerate for at least 1 hour, or until needed.

Meanwhile, make the broth. Put the carcass, stock, ginger, star anise, soy sauce, hoisin sauce and oyster sauce in a pan and bring to the boil. Reduce the heat and simmer for 10 minutes.

Remove the star anise and add the spring onions, garlic, carrots and bamboo shoots. Simmer for 5 minutes more.

Remove the wontons from the fridge and add to the broth in the pan. Once they float to the surface, remove the pan from the heat.

Divide the broth and wontons between 4 individual soup bowls, add the reserved slices of duck breast and serve immediately.

If you have never ventured into making an Asian-inspired soup, this recipe is a good starting point. Egg-flower soup is easy to prepare and totally delicious.

egg-flower soup

1 litre (1¾ pints/4 cups) Asian chicken stock (see p.17) or white chicken stock (see p.17)

300g (10oz) mixed red and yellow cherry tomatoes, cut in half

100g (3½oz/scant ⅔ cup) cooked peas

1 tbsp cornflour

1 tbsp Chinese rice wine or dry sherry

½ tsp sesame oil

2 tsp soy sauce

2 tbsp hoisin sauce

2 tbsp coarsely chopped coriander

sea salt and freshly ground black pepper

2 eggs, lightly beaten

2 spring onions, shredded, to garnish

Put the stock in a large pan and bring to the boil. Add the tomatoes and peas, reduce the heat to low and cook for 1 minute.

In a bowl, mix the cornflour with the rice wine or sherry. Increase the heat under the stock to bring it back to the boil, then stir in the cornflour mixture to thicken it lightly. Add the sesame oil, soy sauce, hoisin sauce and coriander, then remove from the heat. Season to taste with a little salt and pepper.

Pour the beaten eggs into the very hot soup through a fine sieve, stirring continuously. When the egg floats to the top of the soup, remove from the heat. The egg will continue cooking.

Divide the soup between 4 individual soup bowls, scatter with the shredded spring onions and serve immediately.

Variation: Chicken and Sweetcorn Soup Proceed as for the basic soup but omit the eggs, replace the peas with cooked sweetcorn kernels and add shredded steamed chicken breast just before serving.

The ingredients for this soup may seem a little daunting but most, if not all, are readily available in small shops on our multi-cultural high streets or in specialist food shops. You can buy dashi granules, which are used to make the Japanese base stock, in many Asian shops. If you can get hold of them, there is no need to use the kombu and bonito flakes. The finished soup is very fragrant and light – typical of Asian broths and soups in general.

shiitake-enoki miso noodle soup

750ml (1¼ pints/3 cups) water

15cm (6in) piece of kombu

50g (1¾oz) dried bonito flakes

2 tbsp dashi granules (optional – instead of the kombu and bonito flakes)

2 tbsp white miso paste

125g (4½oz/2 cups) shiitake mushrooms, thinly sliced

75g (2½oz) enoki mushrooms

1 tbsp wakame

150g (5½oz) dried soba noodles

1 tbsp nori strips

handful of baby spinach leaves

2 shallots, thinly sliced lengthways

75g (2½oz/½ cup) firm tofu, cubed

2 spring onions, shredded

Prepare a base of dashi stock. Put the water, kombu and bonito flakes in a pan, bring to the boil, then reduce the heat and simmer for 10 minutes. When the kombu and bonito have sunk to the bottom, strain the stock through a fine sieve. Alternatively, add the dashi granules to the boiling water instead of using the kombu and bonito flakes.

Return the strained stock to the pan, bring to the boil, then reduce the heat to the lowest possible. Add the miso paste, shiitake and enoki mushrooms and the wakame. Leave to sweat but do not allow to boil.

Meanwhile, cook the noodles following the packet instructions, then drain. Divide the cooked noodles, nori, spinach, shallots, tofu and spring onions between 4 individual soup bowls, add the miso mushroom broth and serve immediately.

Pho is a traditional Vietnamese favourite. It is a complex, flavourful soup that is often served at breakfast as a hearty start to the day. Traditionally made with beef or chicken, my vegetarian version rings the changes. All the ingredients can be sourced from good Asian delis. I like to make the stock a day in advance as I think the flavour is better.

vegetable pho

1 litre (1¾ pints/4 cups) vegetable stock (see p.22)

3 tbsp soy sauce

4 garlic cloves, crushed

2 tsp caster sugar

2cm (¾in) piece of root ginger, finely grated

2 star anise

½ stick of cinnamon

1 tsp cardamom seeds, cracked

125g (4½oz) rice stick noodles

100g (3½oz/1 cup) beansprouts

½ Chinese cabbage, shredded

1 tbsp finely chopped coriander leaves

75g (2½oz) oyster mushrooms, cut into strips

1 tbsp finely chopped Vietnamese mint (optional)

1 small red or green pepper, cut in half, deseeded and finely shredded

4 spring onions, thinly shredded

1 red chilli, cut into thin rings

To serve

50g (1¾oz/⅓ cup) roasted cashews, coarsely chopped (optional)

2 limes, cut into wedges

The day before it is needed, prepare the broth. Put the stock, soy sauce, garlic, sugar, ginger, star anise, cinnamon and cardamom in a large pan, bring to the boil, then reduce the heat and simmer for 30 minutes. Remove from the heat, allow to cool, then refrigerate overnight.

The next day, put the noodles in a heatproof bowl, cover with boiling water and leave to stand for 15–20 minutes, stirring occasionally, or until the noodles are softened and separate. Drain well and set aside.

Remove the broth from the fridge, strain through a fine sieve into a clean pan and bring to the boil. Add the beansprouts, cabbage, coriander, oyster mushrooms, mint, if using, and the pepper, spring onions and chilli. Reduce the heat and simmer for 2 minutes.

Divide the noodles between 4 individual soup bowls, pour the vegetables and broth over, then scatter with the chopped cashews, if using. Serve immediately. Serve the wedges of lime separately.

Variation: Beef Pho Proceed as for the basic soup but for a meaty version, add 300g (10oz) tender beef fillet, cut into fine slithers or 300g (10oz) thinly sliced skinless chicken or duck breast when adding the vegetables.

COOK'S SECRET _____

Although the ingredients list may seem long, the soup is very easy to make. The broth can be made in advance in bulk and frozen.

While travelling through Thailand some years ago, I took every opportunity to enjoy this spicy broth-based prawn soup. Full of flavour and with both sour and spicy overtones, it is unique among the great soups of South-east Asia. The name derives from *tom*, the broth, while *yum* denotes its sour and spicy flavour. Nam prik pao (roasted chilli paste) can be sourced from Thai stores but red curry paste may be more readily available and can be substituted. Fish and chicken can be used instead of prawns. Some Thai cooks also add a handful of cooked steamed rice to the finished soup.

tom yum goong

Put the oil in a heavy-based frying pan over a medium heat, then add the reserved prawn shells and fry for 4–5 minutes, or until lightly coloured. Add the roasted chilli paste or red curry paste and fry for 2 minutes more.

Add the chicken stock or water, bring to the boil, reduce the heat and simmer for 15 minutes. Do not over-cook or it will dull the flavour of the broth.

Remove from the heat and strain through a fine sieve into a clean pan. Discard the prawn shells.

Add all the remaining ingredients except the prawns, coriander and lime juice. Simmer for 5 minutes to infuse the flavours. Stir in the prawns and cook for 2–3 minutes more.

Add the coriander and lime juice, a little at a time, to taste. Divide between the individual soup bowls and serve immediately.

Variation: Proceed as for the basic soup but for a richer version, add other shellfish, such as scallops, clams or mussels, when adding the prawns.

2 tbsp peanut or vegetable oil

450g (1lb) raw tiger prawns, peeled and deveined, tails intact and shells reserved

2 tbsp nam prik pao (roasted chilli paste) or red curry paste

1.5 litres (2¾ pints/1.3 quarts) white chicken stock (see p.17) or water

2 stalks of lemongrass, tough outer layers removed and the rest finely chopped

2 tbsp tamarind paste

½ tsp ground turmeric

2 small Thai red chillies, finely chopped

2cm (¾in) piece of galangal or root ginger, finely shredded

2 tsp palm sugar or brown sugar

6 kaffir lime leaves, finely shredded

100g (3½oz/1½ cups) shiitake mushrooms, thinly sliced

1 tsp fish sauce (nam pla)

1 tbsp coriander leaves

juice of 1 lime

Another Asian-inspired soup with a wonderfully fragrant broth base, this one is delicately perfumed with cinnamon and aniseed and it also has the added crispiness of the deep-fried pork belly. Traditionally, other offal parts of the pig, such as liver, are also added. I like to serve this soup accompanied by additions that my guests can choose from, so they get a say in the flavours in their bowl.

crispy pork belly soup with pumpkin, star anise and cinnamon

1kg (2¼lb) pork belly, rind on and cut into 1cm (½in) strips

1 tbsp Chinese five-spice powder

1 litre (1¾ pints/4 cups) white chicken stock (see p.17)

100ml (3½fl oz/scant ½ cup) sweet Indonesian soy sauce (ketjap manis)

3 tbsp Chinese rice wine or dry sherry

2 tbsp brown sugar

2.5cm (1in) piece of root ginger, finely grated

2 garlic cloves, crushed

½ cinnamon stick

4 star anise

1 small red chilli, thinly sliced

2 tbsp fish sauce (nam pla)

4 tbsp hoisin sauce

½ cucumber, cut in half horizontally then cut into 1cm (½in) slices

400g (14oz) pumpkin flesh, cut into 2cm (¾in) cubes

200g (7oz) glass (cellophane) noodles

vegetable oil, for deep-frying

3 tbsp coarsely chopped coriander

2 spring onions, shredded

To serve

crispy-fried garlic slices

crispy-fried finely chopped root ginger

The day before, place the pork belly in a large bowl, sprinkle over the five-spice powder and rub it well into the pork. Cover with clingfilm and refrigerate overnight or for at least 4 hours.

The next day, put the pork belly in a large pan and add all the remaining ingredients except the pumpkin, noodles, oil, coriander and spring onions.

Bring to the boil, reduce the heat and simmer for 1½–2 hours, or until the pork is very tender. Skim off any impurities that rise to the surface. About 10 minutes before the pork is cooked, add the pumpkin.

When the pork is cooked, remove it and the pumpkin with a slotted spoon and set aside to cool.

Add the noodles to the broth and simmer for 5 minutes, or until cooked.

Put the oil in a deep pan and heat to 180°C (350°F). Carefully lower the pork into the hot oil and fry until golden and crispy. Remove with a slotted spoon onto kitchen paper to drain.

Divide the soup between 4 individual soup bowls. Add the coriander, spring onions and crispy pork. Top with the crispy garlic slices and crispy ginger or alternatively, serve them on the side for your guests to help themselves.

smooth and creamy

Belgian endive (sometimes known as white chicory) is a member of the chicory family, which includes radicchio, escarole, frisée and curly endive. With its crisp texture and sweet, nutty flavour with a hint of bitterness, it is prized as a winter salad leaf and winter vegetable. The Irish Crozier Blue cheese is an utterly delicious addition, while the salsa adds a nice textural contrast.

caramelised belgian endive and crozier blue soup with winter salsa

450g (1lb) Belgian endive

25g (scant 1oz/2 tbsp) unsalted butter

1 onion, coarsely chopped

1 tbsp light brown sugar

½ tsp thyme leaves

750ml (1¼ pints/3 cups) white chicken stock (see p.17)

100ml (3½fl oz/scant ½ cup) whole milk

100ml (3½fl oz/scant ½ cup) double cream

75g (2½oz) Crozier Blue cheese

juice of ¼ lemon

sea salt and freshly ground black pepper

For the winter salsa

75g (2½oz/½ cup) wild rice

1 Granny Smith apple

75g (2½oz/¾ cup) toasted flaked hazelnuts

50g (1¾oz/⅓ cup) raisins, soaked in warm water and drained

2 tbsp snipped chives

juice of ½ lemon

pinch of ground cinnamon

Firstly start preparing the winter salsa. Bring 500ml (16fl oz/2 cups) water to the boil in a pan, add the rice, reduce the heat and simmer gently for 45 minutes, or until the rice is tender. Drain and set aside.

For the soup, shred the endive finely. Heat a large pan, then add the butter, shredded endive, onion and sugar, stir well and cook for about 8 minutes, or until lightly caramelised. Add the thyme and cook for 1 minute more.

Pour the stock and milk over and bring to the boil. Reduce the heat and simmer for 20 minutes.

Transfer to a blender or use a hand-held stick blender to blitz to a smooth purée. Strain through a fine sieve.

Return to a clean pan and bring to the boil. Add the cream and Blue Crozier cheese and stir until the cheese has melted. Finish with the lemon juice and season to taste.

Meanwhile, complete the salsa. Peel and core the apple and cut into small cubes. Put in a bowl with the cooked rice and the remaining salsa ingredients. Toss well and season to taste.

Divide the soup between 4 individual soup bowls. Top with the salsa and serve immediately.

THIS PAGE: Broccoli Soup with
Anchovy Beignets and Salsa Verde
(recipe page 57)

OPPOSITE: Cauliflower Soup with
Brie Toasties (recipe page 56)

I am not a great lover of cauliflower, especially if it is plainly boiled, but when it is made into cauliflower cheese with an oozy cheese crust, it is a revelation. Cauliflower used in soup is another triumph. This recipe is the best of both worlds – a soup that is an inspired variation of cauliflower cheese.

cauliflower soup with brie toasties

15g (½oz/1 tbsp) unsalted butter

1 onion, coarsely shopped

1 small leek, trimmed and coarsely chopped

1 cauliflower, trimmed and cut into smallish florets, about 400g (14oz) in total

600ml (1 pint/2½ cups) white chicken stock (see p.17)

300ml (10fl oz/1¼ cups) whole milk

100ml (3½fl oz/scant ½ cup) double cream

2 tsp truffle oil

cracked black pepper

For the toasties

15g (½oz/1 tbsp) unsalted butter

4 slices of white bread

100g (3½oz) French Brie, cut into 5mm (¼in) slices

10g (¼oz) fresh or canned truffles, thinly sliced

Firstly make the toasties. Butter both sides of the sliced bread, then top 2 of the slices with overlapping slices of Brie so the bread is covered. Top with the truffle, gently pressing down on it before covering lightly with the remaining slices of bread to form 2 sandwiches. Press down again lightly to compress the filling. Refrigerate until required.

Meanwhile, for the soup, melt the butter in a large pan, add the onion and leek and cook for about 10 minutes over a low heat, or until softened. Add the cauliflower florets and cook for 2–3 minutes more. Pour in the stock and bring to the boil. Add the milk, reduce the heat and simmer for 15–20 minutes, or until the cauliflower is very soft.

Transfer to a blender or use a hand-held stick blender to blitz to a smooth purée. Strain through a fine sieve. Return the soup to a clean pan, bring back to the boil, then stir in the cream and whisk in the truffle oil.

Remove the sandwiches from the fridge. Heat a non-stick frying pan over a low-medium heat, add the sandwiches and fry gently until crisp and golden on both sides. Alternatively, toast under a hot grill. Remove the crusts from both toasties, then cut each into 4 small squares.

Divide the soup between 4 individual soup bowls and serve immediately sprinkled with a little cracked black pepper and with the cheese toasties.

Variations: Cauliflower and Almond Soup Proceed as for the basic soup but replace the milk with the same quantity of almond milk and 75g (2½oz/¾ cup) ground almonds. Blend as before. Finish with 100ml (3½fl oz/scant ½ cup) double cream and garnish with 50g (1¾oz/½ cup) toasted flaked almonds.

Cauliflower, Liquorice and Chervil Soup Proceed as for the basic soup but add 2 tsp liquorice essence or 1 tsp ground liquorice together with the stock and milk. Finish with 100ml (3½fl oz/scant ½ cup) cream and garnish with chervil leaves.

My inspired anchovy beignets and salsa verde lift this version of broccoli soup from the ordinary to the extraordinary. Overcooking broccoli makes it dull and unappetising, so cook it to a minimum to retain its vibrant green colour and fresh taste.

broccoli soup with anchovy beignets and salsa verde

25g (scant 1oz/2 tbsp) unsalted butter

1 onion, coarsely chopped

750ml (1¼ pints/3 cups) vegetable stock (see p.22)

250ml (9fl oz/1 cup) whole milk

400g (14oz) firm broccoli, trimmed and cut into florets and stalks cut into chunks

sea salt and freshly ground black pepper

pinch of freshly grated nutmeg

For the beignets

50g (1¾oz/⅓ cup) plain flour

30g (1oz/1 cup) cornflour

1 tsp baking powder

200ml (7fl oz/¾ cup) iced water

vegetable oil, for deep-frying

20 small white anchovy fillets in olive oil (boquerones)

For the salsa verde

(makes 150ml/5fl oz/⅔ cup)

2 anchovy fillets in oil, drained

1 garlic clove, crushed

juice of ½ lemon

1 tsp baby capers, rinsed and drained

1 tbsp coarsely coarsely chopped flat-leaf parsley

½ tbsp coarsely coarsely chopped mint leaves

½ tsp coarsely coarsely chopped tarragon leaves

75ml (2½fl oz/⅓ cup) extra virgin olive oil

Firstly make the salsa verde. Put all the ingredients in a mini blender and blitz to a slightly coarse purée. Season to taste and set aside. You will only need 75ml (2½fl oz/⅓ cup).

To make the soup, heat the butter in a heavy-based pan, then add the onion and cook over a low heat for about 10 minutes, or until softened. Pour the stock and milk over and bring to the boil. Reduce the heat and add the broccoli florets and stalks. Simmer for 10–12 minutes, or until the vegetables are just tender.

Meanwhile, make the beignets. Put the plain flour and cornflour in a bowl and add the baking powder and enough iced water to form a batter that thinly coats the back of a spoon.

Heat the oil to 180°C (350°F) in a deep pan. Dip the anchovy fillets individually into the prepared batter and deep-fry in the hot oil for 30 seconds until golden and crisp. Remove with a slotted spoon and drain on kitchen paper. Season liberally with sea salt and set aside.

Transfer the soup to a blender or use a hand-held stick blender to blitz to a smooth purée. Strain through a fine sieve and season to taste with salt, pepper and nutmeg.

Divide the soup between 4 individual soup bowls. Top each with a pile of crispy anchovy fillets and a drizzle of the salsa verde. Serve immediately.

Variation: Broccoli Soup with Davidstow Cheddar Proceed as for the basic soup but top with fried or baked croûtons sprinkled with freshly grated Davidstow Cheddar cheese.

This lovely winter-inspired soup is made from one of my favourite and, in my opinion, one of the most underrated vegetables – celeriac or celery root. It must be its appearance that puts people off; it certainly cannot be its deliciously nutty celery-like taste. The addition of the smoked almond butter is an unusual and subtle touch while the crispy-fried celeriac slices add an interesting texture.

celery root soup with two textures and smoked butter

25g (scant 1oz/2 tbsp) unsalted butter

1 onion, coarsely chopped

450g (1lb/2¾ cups) celeriac, peeled and cut into chunks

2 Comice pears, peeled, cored and cut into chunks

1 litre (1¾ pints/4 cups) white chicken stock (see p.17)

120ml (4fl oz/½ cup) double cream

sea salt and freshly ground black pepper

For the smoked almond butter

75g (2½oz/½ cup) smoked almonds

50g (1¾oz/3½ tbsp) unsalted or smoked butter

1 tsp hickory-smoked essence (optional)

1 tbsp lemon juice

For the celeriac crisps

1 small celeriac, peeled and cut into quarters

vegetable oil, for deep-frying

The day before, make the smoked almond butter. Put the almonds, butter, hickory-smoked essence, if using, and lemon juice in a small blender and blitz to a smooth paste. Transfer to a bowl, cover with clingfilm and refrigerate overnight. Alternatively, you can make the smoked almond butter in advance, keep it in the freezer and remove it 10 minutes before needed.

To make the soup, heat the butter in a large pan over a medium heat, then add the onion, celeriac and 100ml (3½fl oz/scant ½ cup) water. Cover with a lid, reduce the heat to low and cook for 10 minutes, or until the vegetables are softened.

Add the pears, mix well, then pour on the stock and half the cream. Simmer gently for 20 minutes, or until the celeriac is tender and soft. Transfer to a blender or use a hand-held stick blender to blitz until smooth and creamy. Strain through a fine sieve and return to a clean pan. Set aside.

Meanwhile, make the celeriac crisps. Use a small hand-held mandolin to slice the celeriac into 6mm (¼in) slices. Heat the oil to 180°C (350°F) in a deep pan, then add the celeriac and fry for 30–40 seconds, or until crisp and golden. You may need to do this in batches.

Remove with a slotted spoon onto kitchen paper and drain well. Season liberally with sea salt and set aside.

Return the soup to a clean pan and bring to the boil. Remove from the heat and whisk in the smoked almond butter, a little at a time, or until the soup is smooth and creamy. Season to taste.

Divide the soup between 4 individual soup bowls, garnish with the celeriac crisps and serve immediately.

Variation: Celery Root Soup with Horseradish Crème Fraîche
Proceed as for the basic soup, increasing the quantity of celeriac to 600g (1lb 5oz) and omitting the pears. Blend the soup and garnish with a dollop of horseradish crème fraîche made by mixing together 2 tbsp horseradish cream with 4 tbsp crème fraîche.

sardinian chickpea and fennel soup

I first tasted this soup in Sardinia. I was in a restaurant overlooking the beautiful coastline of Porto Cervo on the Costa Smeralda, a haven for many rich travellers whose large yachts were moored nearby. Wild fennel is not readily available and normal Florence fennel doesn't do the trick, so instead substitute some lightly toasted fennel seeds.

white onion soup with cider and thyme

I recommend Italian or English white onions for this soup: they are more flavourful and give a better yield than Spanish onions, which are often bruised and soft. Make a meal of this by serving with plenty of chunky baguette bread.

pumpkin and walnut soup with cèpes

This creamy soup topped with rich, earthy wild mushrooms is ideal for a winter's evening dinner party. If you can't find fresh cèpes or porcini, dried ones make a worthy substitute.

creamed pea soup with curry

Pea soup with curry may sound a strange combination but please try it. I know you will love it. The garnish of fresh pea shoots adds a real seasonal feel to this soup.

OPPOSITE Top left: Sardinian Chickpea and Fennel Soup (recipe page 62); top right: White Onion Soup with Cider and Thyme (recipe page 62); bottom left: Pumpkin and Walnut Soup with Cèpes (recipe page 63); bottom right: Creamed Pea Soup with Curry (recipe page 63)

sardinian chickpea and fennel soup

350g (12oz/2 cups) dried chickpeas, soaked overnight, then drained

75g (2½oz) wild fennel, trimmed and coarsely chopped or 2 tsp fennel seeds, lightly toasted

1.5 litres (2¾ pints/1.3 quarts) white chicken stock (see p.17)

3 tbsp extra virgin olive oil

1 onion, coarsely chopped

2 garlic cloves, crushed

1 carrot, coarsely chopped

juice of ½ lemon

½ tsp lemon zest

few toasted fennel seeds, to garnish

Put the soaked chickpeas in a large pan, cover with water and bring to the boil. Reduce the heat and simmer for 1 hour, or until tender. Rinse in a colander under cold running water and set 4 tbsp aside.

Put the remaining chickpeas in a clean pan, add the wild fennel or fennel seeds, cover with the stock and bring to the boil. Reduce the heat to a simmer.

Meanwhile, in another pan, heat 1 tbsp of the oil over a medium heat, then add the onion, garlic and carrot, reduce the heat to low and cook for about 10 minutes, or until softened. Add to the chickpeas in their pan and cook 20 minutes more.

Transfer to a blender or use a hand-held stick blender to blitz to a smooth purée. If the soup is too thick add more stock or a little water. Return the soup to a clean pan.

Make the lemon oil by heating the remaining 2 tbsp oil in a small pan over a low heat, then add the lemon juice and zest. Reduce the heat as low as possible and infuse for 2 minutes.

Bring the soup to the boil and add the reserved chickpeas. Divide between 4 individual soup bowls, drizzle with a little of the lemon oil, sprinkle over the toasted fennel seeds and serve immediately.

white onion soup with cider and thyme

50g (1¾oz/3½ tbsp) unsalted butter

450g (1lb) Italian or English onions, coarsely chopped

2 tsp thyme leaves, plus extra to garnish

1 garlic clove, crushed

1 litre (1¾ pints/4 cups) white chicken stock (see p.17)

150ml (5fl oz/⅔ cup) dry cider

100ml (3½fl oz/scant ½ cup) single cream

sea salt and freshly ground black pepper

pinch of caster sugar

Heat half the butter in a large pan over a gentle heat, then add the onion, thyme and garlic and cook for 15–20 minutes, or until the onions are softened. Pour the stock and cider over and bring to the boil. Reduce the heat and simmer for 15 minutes more.

Transfer to a blender or use a hand-held stick blender to blitz to a smooth purée. Strain through a fine sieve and return to a clean pan. Add 75ml (2½fl oz/⅓ cup) of the cream, the salt and pepper and a pinch of sugar to help balance the acidity of the onions.

Bring to almost boiling point, then divide between 4 individual soup bowls. Drizzle with the remaining cream, sprinkle over some extra thyme leaves and serve immediately.

Variation: White Onion and Lovage Soup Proceed as for the basic soup, omitting the thyme but adding 2 tbsp shredded lovage leaves to the soup before serving.

pumpkin and walnut soup with cèpes

400g (14oz) pumpkin (peeled weight; preferably iron bark pumpkin), peeled and cut into 5cm (2in) pieces

3 tbsp extra virgin olive oil

25g (scant 1oz/2 tbsp) unsalted butter

1 onion, coarsely chopped

75g (2½oz/¾ cup) walnut halves

750ml (1¼ pints/3 cups) white chicken stock (see p.17)

100ml (3½fl oz/scant ½ cup) dry Madeira

100ml (3½fl oz/scant ½ cup) double cream

200ml (7fl oz/¾ cup) whole milk

200g (7oz/3 cups) fresh cèpes, cleaned and sliced

1 shallot, finely chopped

1 garlic clove, crushed

sea salt and freshly ground black pepper

2 tbsp snipped chives, to garnish

Preheat the oven to 150°C (300°F/Gas 2). Put the pumpkin pieces in a roasting tin, drizzle with 2 tbsp of the oil and roast in the preheated oven for 40 minutes, turning occasionally until tender and golden. Set aside.

Heat a large pan over a medium heat, then add half the butter, the onion and the walnuts. Stir well, reduce the heat to low and cook for 10 minutes. Add the roasted pumpkin, stock and Madeira. Bring to the boil, then reduce the heat and simmer for 20 minutes.

Add the cream and milk, then transfer to a blender or use a hand-held stick blender to blitz to a smooth paste. Strain through a fine sieve, return to a clean pan and bring to the boil again.

Meanwhile, heat the remaining oil in a frying pan, then add the cèpes, shallot and garlic and stir well. Fry quickly until golden brown, then whisk in the remaining butter and season to taste.

Divide the soup between 4 individual soup bowls, top with the cèpes, sprinkle over the chives and serve immediately.

creamed pea soup with curry

25g (scant 1oz/2 tbsp) unsalted butter

1 onion, coarsely chopped

1 round lettuce, leaves separated and washed

2 tsp mild curry powder

1 litre (1¾ pints/4 cups) white chicken stock (see p.17)

400g (14oz/3½ cups) fresh (podded weight) or frozen peas

1 tbsp flat-leaf parsley, leaves only

100ml (3½fl oz/scant ½ cup) double cream

sea salt and freshly ground black pepper

To garnish

10g (¼oz) pea shoots

50g (1¾oz/1⅔ cups) bread croûtons (see p.11)

Heat the butter in a large pan over a medium heat, then add the onion and cook for 10 minutes, or until softened. Coarsely chop the lettuce, add to the pan and cook for 2 minutes, or until the leaves have wilted.

Stir in the curry powder and cook for 1 minute. Pour the stock over, increase the heat and bring to the boil. Add the peas and parsley and bring back to the boil quickly. Reduce the heat and simmer for just 10 minutes to retain their freshness.

Transfer to a blender or use a hand-held stick blender to blitz to a smooth purée. Strain through a fine sieve. Return the soup to a clean pan, add the cream and season to taste. Bring to the boil.

Divide the soup between 4 individual soup bowls and garnish with the pea shoots and croûtons. Serve immediately.

Variation: Pea Soup with Garlic and Parmesan Cream

Proceed as for the basic soup, omitting the curry powder but adding 2 peeled garlic cloves when you add the peas and parsley. Put 2 tbsp freshly grated Parmesan cheese and 100ml (3½fl oz/scant ½ cup) double cream in a bowl, mix together, then whisk quickly into the hot soup. Garnish with the pea shoots but omit the croûtons.

Roasting peppers and aubergines gives them a wonderfully sweet yet smoky flavour. With its saffron aïoli and hint of thyme, this soup is sure to remind you of sun-filled Mediterranean holidays.

roasted pepper and aubergine soup with saffron aïoli

3 large red peppers, deseeded and cut into large pieces

1 large aubergine, cut into 2.5cm (1in) cubes

2 garlic cloves, unpeeled

2 tbsp extra virgin olive oil

30g (1oz/2 tbsp) unsalted butter

1 large onion, coarsely chopped

1 tsp smoked paprika

1 tbsp finely chopped thyme

200ml (7fl oz/¾ cup) passata or tomato juice

2 tsp caster sugar

750ml (1¼ pints/3 cups) white chicken stock (see p.17)

60ml (2fl oz/¼ cup) double cream

sea salt and freshly ground black pepper

For the saffron aïoli

½ tsp fresh saffron strands

100ml (3½fl oz/scant ½ cup) good-quality mayonnaise

1 garlic clove, crushed

To serve

8 slices of baguette, toasted

a little paprika

Preheat the oven to 200°C (400°F/Gas 6). Put the peppers, aubergine and garlic in a roasting tin, drizzle with the oil and put in the preheated oven. Roast for 30 minutes, or until the peppers are softened and slightly charred. Check from time to time that the garlic does not burn; it may be necessary to remove it a little sooner.

Meanwhile, heat half the butter in a heavy-based pan over a medium heat, then add the onion and cook for 5–8 minutes, or until the onion is softened. Stir in the paprika and thyme and cook for 5 minutes, then add the roasted peppers, aubergine and garlic, followed by the passata or tomato juice, sugar and stock.

Bring to the boil then reduce the heat and simmer for 30 minutes, or until the vegetables are softened.

Meanwhile, prepare the aïoli. Heat 3 tbsp water in a small pan and add the saffron. Reduce the heat as low as possible and leave to infuse for 2–3 minutes. Remove from the heat and leave to cool completely.

Add the saffron and its liquid to the mayonnaise in a bowl. Stir in the garlic and season to taste. Set aside.

Transfer the soup to a blender or use a hand-held stick blender to blitz to a smooth purée. Strain through a fine sieve. Return the soup to a clean pan, bring to the boil and stir in the cream. Whisk in the remaining butter and season to taste.

Divide the soup between 4 individual soup bowls and serve with the toasted baguette and saffron aïoli sprinkled with a little paprika.

Fresh broad beans in season are a real treat. When they are young, you can simply strip them of their skins and serve them raw seasoned with sea salt, or you can make them into a soup like this one. As the season progresses, the skins become thicker and tougher, so peeling them is absolutely necessary. However, in this case, as the soup is liquidised, there is no need to peel them whatever their age.

breton artichoke and broad bean soup with marjoram

8 baby artichokes (poivrades)

juice of ½ lemon

350g (12oz) young broad beans (podded weight)

1 tbsp extra virgin olive oil

2 shallots, coarsely chopped

1 tsp coarsely chopped fresh marjoram or ½ tsp dried marjoram

750ml (1¼ pints/3 cups) white chicken stock (see p.17) or vegetable stock (see p.22)

1 tsp caster sugar

60ml (2fl oz/¼ cup) crème fraîche

15g (½oz/1 tbsp) unsalted butter, chilled and cut into small pieces

10g (¼oz) marjoram leaves, to garnish

Prepare the artichokes. Snap off the stalks and peel away the few tough outer green leaves until you reach the inner light-green heart. As you prepare each artichoke, drop it into a bowl of water acidulated with the lemon juice to stop the artichoke from discolouring. Set aside.

Bring a pan of water to the boil, add the beans, reduce the heat and simmer for 5 minutes. Drain and set aside.

Heat the oil in a pan over a medium heat, then add the shallots and marjoram. Reduce the heat to low and cook for 2 minutes, or until softened.

Drain the artichokes and cut in half. Remove the hairy choke, or centre, from each. If the artichokes are young enough, there should not be much choke. Add the artichokes to the shallots in the pan, then add the beans, stock and sugar, increase the heat and bring to the boil.

Reduce the heat and simmer for 20–25 minutes, or until the artichokes are tender. Transfer to a blender or use a hand-held stick blender to blitz to a smooth purée. Strain through a fine sieve to remove any fibres.

Return to a clean pan and add the crème fraîche and butter. Whisk until smooth.

Divide the soup between 4 individual soup bowls, scatter with the marjoram leaves and serve immediately.

Orange sweet potatoes (kumara) have risen in status over the years and are now somewhat trendy. They are sweet, full of flavour and nutrients, and make a tasty alternative to the great British potato. This recipe is mildly spicy and exotic.

kumara, lime and ginger soup

1 tbsp sunflower oil

750g (1lb 10oz) orange sweet potato, peeled and cut into chunks

1 onion, coarsely chopped

1 garlic clove, crushed

2cm (¾in) piece of root ginger, grated

450ml (15fl oz/2 cups) vegetable stock (see p.22)

250ml (9fl oz/1 cup) coconut milk

juice and grated zest of 1 small lime

100ml (3½fl oz/scant ½ cup) double cream

sea salt and freshly ground black pepper

Heat the oil in a large pan over a low-medium heat, then add the sweet potato and cook for 5 minutes, or until the potato begins to soften. Add the onion, garlic and ginger, cover with a lid and cook for 10 minutes more.

Pour the stock and coconut milk over and bring to the boil, then reduce the heat and simmer for 15 minutes. Transfer to a blender or use a hand-held stick blender to blitz to a smooth purée. Strain through a fine sieve.

Return to the clean pan and bring back to the boil. Remove from the heat, then add the lime juice, half the zest and 50ml (scant 2fl oz/¼ cup) of the cream.

Season to taste. Divide the soup between 4 individual soup bowls, swirl over the remaining cream, add the remaining zest and serve immediately.

Variations: Sweet Potato Soup with Pesto and Crispy Chorizo
Proceed as for the basic soup, replacing the coconut milk with whole milk and omitting the lime zest and juice. Serve drizzled with pesto (see p.163) and topped with crispy-fried thinly sliced cooking chorizo.

Sweet Potato and Nutmeg Soup Proceed as for the basic soup but using 750ml (1¼ pints/3 cups) vegetable stock (see p.22) and omitting the coconut milk, lime juice and zest. After blending, season with salt, pepper and nutmeg to taste.

When knobbly Jerusalem artichokes hit the markets in early autumn, this soup is one of the dishes I rush to make. The slightly strange-looking vegetable enjoys its well-deserved culinary status. My soup is a feast for the eyes with its garnish of herbs and flowers. It is equally delicious served hot or cold.

jerusalem artichoke soup with saffron and herbs and flowers

375g (13oz) Jerusalem artichokes

juice of ½ lemon

50g (1¾oz/3½ tbsp) unsalted butter

1 onion, coarsely chopped

1 garlic clove, crushed

1 tsp thyme leaves

100ml (3½fl oz/scant ½ cup) whole milk

good pinch of fresh saffron strands

250ml (9fl oz/1 cup) hot white chicken stock (see p.17) or hot vegetable stock (see p.22)

100ml (3½fl oz/scant ½ cup) double cream

sea salt and freshly ground black pepper

your choice of herbs (such as baby basil cress, coriander cress or parsley leaves) and flowers (such as dandelions, borage and pansies), to garnish

Peel and cube the artichokes and put them in a bowl of water, acidulated with the lemon juice to stop them from discolouring. Set aside.

Heat the butter over a medium heat in a heavy-based pan, then add the onion, garlic and thyme and cook, stirring occasionally, for 10 minutes, or until the onions are softened.

Meanwhile, heat the milk in a small pan, then add the saffron and bring to the boil. Reduce the heat and simmer for 5 minutes to infuse the milk with the saffron.

Drain the artichokes. Pour the infused milk onto the softened onion and add the artichokes and hot stock. Bring to the boil, cover, then reduce the heat and simmer for 15–20 minutes, or until the artichokes are tender.

Transfer to a blender or use a hand-held stick blender to blitz to a smooth purée. Strain through a fine sieve. Return to a clean pan, bring back to the boil, add the cream and season to taste.

Divide the soup between the individual soup bowls and garnish with your choice of herbs and flowers. Serve immediately.

Variation: Roasted Jerusalem Artichoke Soup Roast the Jerusalem artichokes with 150g (5½oz/¾ cup) cubed bacon and 1 tsp thyme for 30 minutes in a preheated oven at 160°C (325°F/Gas 3) until golden. Put the roasted artichokes in a pan over a medium heat and add 250g (9oz/1 cup) peeled and cubed potatoes. Cover with the stock, as in the basic recipe and cook until tender. Transfer to a blender or use a hand-held stick blender to blitz to a smooth purée. Strain through a fine sieve, then finish with the cream.

In recent years there has been a growing interest in foraging for just about everything, from sea herbs and wild flowers to wild mushrooms. The interest in wild food is definitely on the up; there are even courses run by experts and great online sites that help with identification. That means there are no excuses, so get your boots on and head for the woods. But if you are not willing to indulge your hunter-gatherer instincts, there is a great variety of mushrooms available in shops and delis. Do not be surprised by the use of cacao in this recipe. As you'll discover, it enhances the natural earthy flavour of the mushrooms.

creamed wild mushroom soup with cacao

25g (scant 1oz/2 tbsp) unsalted butter

2 shallots, coarsely chopped

1 garlic clove, crushed

500g (1lb 2oz) wild mushrooms (your own selection or what you manage to discover)

1 tbsp plain flour

750ml (1¼ pints/3 cups) white chicken stock (see p.17)

100ml (3½fl oz/scant ½ cup) whole milk

2 sprigs of thyme

75ml (2½fl oz/⅓ cup) Madeira

75ml (2½fl oz/⅓ cup) whipping cream

2 tsp unsweetened cacao powder

sea salt and freshly ground black pepper

Heat the butter in a heavy-based pan over a medium heat, then add the shallots and garlic and cook for 2–3 minutes, or until softened.

Meanwhile, wash the mushrooms thoroughly under a little running water. Do not soak them as they will absorb the water and become spongy. Add the mushrooms to the pan, increase the heat and fry for 2–3 minutes, or until they are lightly browned and no liquid remains.

Sprinkle over the flour and mix well, then reduce the heat to low and stir with a wooden spoon to make a roux around the mushrooms. Cook, stirring continuously for 2 minutes, or until the flour is cooked and the roux and mushrooms are well mixed together.

Add the stock, milk and thyme and bring to the boil. Reduce the heat and simmer for 20 minutes. Add the Madeira, cook for 5 minutes more, then use a slotted spoon to remove some of the mushrooms from the pan. Set aside for garnishing the soup.

Transfer the mixture in the pan to a blender or use a hand-held stick blender to blitz to a smooth purée. If you want a smoother soup, strain it through a fine sieve.

Whip the cream until it forms soft peaks. Add half the cacao and the whipped cream to the soup then, using a hand-held stick blender, whisk until the soup becomes light and airy. Season to taste.

Divide the reserved mushrooms between 4 individual soup bowls and pour the soup over. Sprinkle with the remaining cacao and serve immediately.

creamed wild mushroom soup | **73**

how to make the perfect

asparagus velouté with spring morels

In spring, we chefs eagerly await the arrival of British asparagus, which is in season between late May and June. Oh dear, why is it such a short season? At the same time, fresh morels appear, making them the ideal partner for the asparagus. If fresh morels are not available, substitute dried morels, reconstituted in water for 30 minutes. This recipe teaches you the basics of making a velouté – a puréed soup thickened with eggs and cream. You can apply the same principles to any other velouté.

600g (1lb 5oz) green asparagus spears, peeled and woody part of the stem discarded, or the same amount, drained weight, of canned green asparagus spears

750ml (1¼ pints/3 cups) white chicken stock (see p.17) or vegetable stock (see p.22)

250ml (9fl oz/1 cup) whole milk

25g (scant 1oz/2 tbsp) unsalted butter

2 tbsp plain flour

2 egg yolks

100ml (3½fl oz/scant ½ cup) double cream

100g (3½oz) fresh morels, washed to remove any sand and chopped into small pieces or 30g (1oz/²/₃ cup) dried morels, soaked in hot water for 30 minutes, squeezed to remove excess water and chopped into small pieces

sea salt and freshly ground black pepper

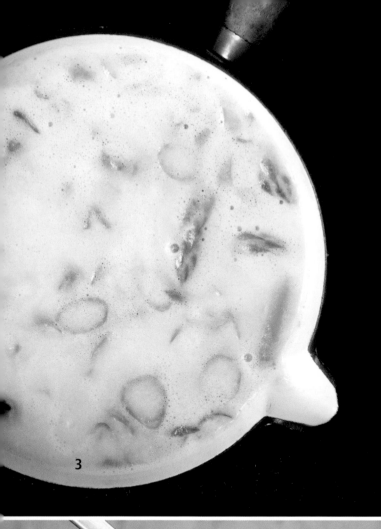

3

1 Cut the asparagus into short lengths. Put in a pan over a medium heat with the stock and the milk and cook for 15 minutes, or until just soft. Drain and set aside, reserving the cooking liquid.

2 Heat the butter in a large pan over a low heat. Add the flour and stir with a wooden spoon to make a roux. Cook, stirring continuously for 2 minutes, or until the flour is cooked.

3 Gradually whisk in the reserved cooking liquid, a little at a time, whisking continuously. Simmer for 15 minutes. Add the cooked asparagus and cook for 10 minutes more.

4 Transfer to a blender or use a hand-held stick blender.

5 Blitz to a smooth purée.

COOK'S SECRET
To remove the woody base of the asparagus spear, after peeling, hold it between your two hands and bend it sharply. The woody base will snap off at this point, leaving the best eating part.

4

5

6 Strain the soup through a sieve into a clean pan.

7 Bring the soup to the boil. Meanwhile, whisk together the egg yolks and cream in a bowl. then gradually pour the boiling soup onto the egg-cream mixture in the bowl.

8 Return the contents of the bowl to the pan, add the chopped morels and reduce the heat to low. Whisk well continuously, remove the soup from the heat just before it comes to the boil, then season to taste. Divide between 4 individual soup bowls and serve immediately.

Variation: White Asparagus and Herb Soup

Proceed as for the basic soup but use white asparagus instead of green and omit the morels. Before serving, add 1 tsp each finely chopped tarragon, chervil and chives. Add 1 tsp lemon juice just before serving.

This delightful tomato soup is simple to make and is redolent of the freshness of summer. Puréeing it in a blender makes the colour paler and less appealing, so I always recommend straining it through a coarse sieve instead. The accompanying olive tapenade straws add to the summery effect.

vine tomato velouté with olive tapenade straws

25g (scant 1oz/2 tbsp) unsalted butter

1 large onion, thinly sliced

800g (1¾lb) ripe vine tomatoes, cut into quarters

10 sprigs of basil

2 garlic cloves, crushed

2 sprigs of thyme

1 tbsp caster sugar

200ml (7fl oz/¾ cup) tomato juice

750ml (1¼ pints/3 cups) white chicken stock (see p.17)

150ml (5fl oz/⅔ cup) whipping or double cream

2 egg yolks

sea salt and freshly ground black pepper

1 tbsp pesto (see p.163)

8–12 olive tapenade straws (see p.12), to serve

Heat the butter in a large pan, then add the onion and cook over a low heat for 10 minutes, or until softened. Add the tomatoes, basil, garlic, thyme and sugar. Continue cooking over a low heat for 15 minutes, or until the tomatoes are softened and pulpy in texture.

Increase the heat, add the tomato juice and stock and bring to the boil. Reduce the heat and simmer for 10–15 minutes.

Strain through a coarse sieve, pressing down on the mixture with a small ladle to extract as much liquid as possible. Return the soup to a clean pan and bring to the boil.

Meanwhile, whisk the cream and egg yolks together in a large bowl. When the soup reaches boiling point, pour it gradually onto the egg-cream mixture, whisking quickly and continuously.

Return the contents of the bowl to the pan, put over a low heat and cook, whisking continuously. Just before the soup reaches boiling point, remove the pan from the heat and season to taste.

Divide the soup between the individual soup bowls and drizzle each with 1 tsp pesto. Serve immediately with the olive tapenade straws.

Variation: Tomato Soup with Balsamic Vinegar and Rocket Oil
Proceed as for the basic soup but add 1 tbsp balsamic vinegar at the same time as the sugar and lightly caramelise them together before adding the tomato juice and stock. In a blender, make some rocket oil by blitzing together a handful of rocket leaves and 75ml (2½fl oz/⅓ cup) extra virgin olive oil. Drizzle each soup with a little of the rocket oil, then serve.

A well-made watercress soup in all its simplicity can be the ultimate in soup-making. Whether served hot or cold, it is delicious, slightly peppery and vibrant green. In fact, it is a real winner on all fronts. Ensure your watercress is of the utmost freshness and beautifully green.

watercress soup

25g (scant 1oz/2 tbsp) unsalted butter

1 onion, coarsely chopped

1 small leek, trimmed and cubed

2 medium potatoes

750ml (1¼ pints/3 cups) vegetable stock (see p.22)

300ml (10fl oz/1¼ cups) whole milk

400g (14oz) watercress, leaves and stalks separated

sea salt and freshly ground black pepper

2 tbsp crème fraîche, to serve

Heat the butter in a large pan over a medium heat, then add the onion and leek. Reduce the heat to low and cook for 10 minutes, or until softened.

Peel and cube the potatoes. Add the stock and milk to the onion and leek mixture and bring to the boil. Add the cubed potatoes and watercress stalks, reduce the heat and simmer for 20 minutes, or until the potatoes are softened.

Add the watercress leaves and mix well. Transfer to a blender or use a hand-held stick blender to blitz to a smooth purée. Strain through a fine sieve and season to taste.

Divide between 4 individual soup bowls and swirl some crème fraîche into each or serve it separately if you prefer. Serve immediately.

Variations: Curried Watercress Soup Proceed as for the basic soup, adding 2 level tsp curry powder at the same time as the onion and leek.

Watercress and Gorgonzola Soup Proceed as for the basic soup, adding 50g (1¾oz/⅓ cup) crumbled Gorgonzola cheese to the soup just before serving.

COOK'S SECRET _____

Adding the watercress leaves just before blending keeps the colour of the soup vibrant and, more importantly, the flavour fresh-tasting.

Sweet scallops and crispy-fried bacon are a marriage made in heaven. The combination makes this soup a wonderful and simple-to-prepare dinner-party starter.

sweetcorn soup with scallops and crispy bacon bits

4 large corn on the cob, outer husks removed

300ml (10fl oz/1¼ cups) whole milk

200ml (7fl oz/¾ cup) double cream

450ml (15fl oz/2 cups) white chicken stock (see p.17)

25g (scant 1oz/2 tbsp) unsalted butter

1 onion, coarsely chopped

2 tbsp plain flour

sea salt and freshly ground black pepper

To garnish

2 tbsp extra virgin olive oil

8 small to medium scallops, removed from their shells and cleaned

75g (2½oz) rashers of streaky bacon, cut into small cubes

2 tbsp snipped chives

Hold each corn on the cob upright on a work surface and remove the kernels with a knife by cutting downwards from top to bottom, leaving the central stem bare.

Bring the kernels to the boil in a pan with the milk, cream and stock, then reduce the heat and simmer for 20–25 minutes, or until the kernels are tender. Drain, reserving the cooking liquid.

Melt the butter in another pan over a low heat, then add the onion and cook for 5 minutes, or until softened. Add the flour and stir with a wooden spoon to make a roux. Cook, stirring continuously for 2 minutes, or until the flour is cooked.

Add the reserved cooking liquid a little at a time, stirring continuously until the mixture has thickened. Reduce the heat and simmer gently for 20 minutes.

Return the cooked kernels to the soup, then transfer to a blender or use a hand-held stick blender to blitz to a smooth purée. Strain through a fine sieve and season to taste.

Meanwhile, heat the oil in a large non-stick frying pan, cut each scallop into 3 slices, then add to the pan and fry for 30–60 seconds on each side, or until golden. Remove with a slotted spoon onto a plate and cover with foil to keep warm.

Add the bacon to the pan and cook for 2–3 minutes, or until crisp, golden and caramelised.

Divide the soup between 4 individual soup bowls and top each with 6 slices of scallop and some bacon. Sprinkle with chives and serve immediately.

Variation: Sweetcorn and Lemongrass Soup To add a lovely lemony tang to the soup, omit the bacon but add 2 stalks of lemongrass, tough outer layers removed and the rest coarsely chopped, to the milk, cream and stock, then proceed as for the basic soup.

THIS PAGE: Roast Chicken Soup
(recipe page 86)

OPPOSITE: Jersey Royal Potato, Wild
Garlic and Cockle Soup (recipe page 87)

Roasting the chicken before adding it to the base soup adds a welcoming burst and intense depth of chicken flavour. Another attraction of this soup is that you can start it from scratch or use leftover pieces and trimmings of roast chicken. I like to add a few thyme leaves before serving.

roast chicken soup

1.5kg (3lb 3oz) free-range roasting chicken

few sprigs of thyme, plus 10g (¼oz) thyme leaves

2 tbsp extra virgin olive oil

sea salt and freshly ground black pepper

50g (1¾oz/3½ tbsp) unsalted butter

50g (1¾oz/⅓ cup) plain flour

1.5 litres (2¾ pints/1.3 quarts) white chicken stock (see p.17)

120ml (4fl oz/½ cup) whole milk

120ml (4fl oz/½ cup) single cream

Preheat the oven to 200°C (400°F/Gas 6). Put the chicken in a roasting tin, tuck the sprigs of thyme inside the cavity of the chicken, drizzle with oil and season liberally with salt.

Put in the preheated oven and roast for 1–1¼ hours, or until cooked through. Baste occasionally with the cooking juices to keep the bird juicy and moist. Remove the chicken from the oven and leave until cool enough to handle.

Meanwhile, heat the butter in a large pan over a low heat. Add the flour and stir with a wooden spoon to make a roux. Cook, stirring continuously for 2 minutes, or until the flour is cooked and the roux turns a light blonde colour.

Add the stock a little at a time, whisking continuously until the mixture is smooth and creamy. Reduce the heat and simmer gently for 10–15 minutes.

Meanwhile, cut the chicken into 2 leg joints and 2 breast joints, then remove the skin from each piece and cut the flesh into 1cm (½in) cubes.

Add the roasted carcass bones to the soup, together with the milk and cream. Simmer gently for 15 minutes more.

Strain the soup through a fine sieve. If the soup is too thick – it should be the consistency of single cream – you may need to add a little more stock. Stir the pieces of cooked chicken into the soup with a few thyme leaves, then season to taste with salt and pepper. Bring back to the boil.

Divide the soup between the individual soup bowls and serve immediately.

Variations: You can make some simple variations to the soup, simply by adding 3 tbsp finely chopped sorrel or parsley, or a small bunch of watercress, leaves only, or 175g (6oz/2½ cups) finely sliced button mushrooms, stewed in milk and drained. You can use the stewing milk to replace the milk in the soup recipe.

Sengalese Chicken Soup Proceed as for the basic soup but add 1 tbsp mild curry powder when you add the milk and cream.

Ever since I got married over 30 years ago, I have lived in and around Essex, a stone's throw from Leigh-on-Sea where, reputedly, the best cockles are found. I love all shellfish but cockles, with their slightly briny flavour, are among my favourites. Here is a great soup using cockles. Frozen ones are available from good fishmongers if you can't find fresh, but the flavour in no way compares with fresh ones. You could use clams or mussels instead if you wish.

jersey royal potato, wild garlic and cockle soup

2kg (4½lb) fresh or frozen cockles in their shells

750ml (1¼ pints/3 cups) hot fish stock (see p.24)

25g (scant 1oz/2 tbsp) unsalted butter

1 large leek, trimmed and shredded

400g (14oz) Jersey Royal or other new potatoes

100ml (3½fl oz/scant ½ cup) double cream

100ml (3½fl oz/scant ½ cup) whole milk

45g (1½oz) wild garlic leaves

1 tbsp lemon juice

sea salt and freshly ground black pepper

Clean the cockles and put them in a large pan. Add 200ml (7fl oz/¾ cup) of the hot stock, cover with a tight-fitting lid and cook for 2–3 minutes over a medium heat, or until the cockles have opened. Drain, reserving the juices. Set aside.

Heat the butter in another large pan over a medium heat, then add the leek and cook for about 5 minutes, or until softened.

Peel and cut the potatoes in half, then add to the pan with the remaining fish stock, the reserved juices from the cockles, the cream and the milk. Bring to the boil, then reduce the heat and simmer for 15–20 minutes, or until the potatoes are tender.

Meanwhile, remove the cockles from their shells and add half to the soup. Transfer the soup to a blender or use a hand-held stick blender to blitz to a smooth purée. Strain through a fine sieve and return the soup to a clean pan.

Shred the wild garlic leaves into strips, add to the pan and return the soup to the boil. Add the remaining cooked cockles and the lemon juice and adjust the seasoning. Divide between the individual soup bowls and serve immediately.

Variation: Welsh Cockle and Laver Bread Soup Proceed as for the basic soup, omitting the garlic leaves and instead adding 100g (3½oz) Welsh laver bread to the soup 5 minutes before the end of the cooking. Transfer to a blender or use a hand-held stick blender to blitz to a smooth purée. Strain through a fine sieve and whisk in 15g (½oz/1 tbsp) chilled unsalted butter and a squeeze of fresh lemon juice before serving.

When I created this soup, I had a classic Italian speciality in mind – squash-filled ravioli with sage butter, sprinkled with crushed almond biscuit and Parmesan cheese. Hence this soup using the same ingredients. It is subtly sweet yet savoury at the same time – and it is very moreish.

butternut squash and almond soup with amaretti and parmesan crumble

25g (scant 1oz/2 tbsp) unsalted butter

1 onion, coarsely chopped

6 sage leaves, coarsely chopped

1 small butternut squash, peeled and cut into chunks

50g (1¾oz/⅓ cup) whole blanched almonds

1.5 litres (2¾ pints/1.3 quarts) white chicken stock (see p.17)

100ml (3½fl oz/scant ½ cup) single cream

To garnish

50g (1¾oz) amaretti biscuits, coarsely crushed

3 tbsp freshly grated Parmesan cheese

Heat the butter in a heavy-based pan, then add the onion and sage and cook for 10 minutes, or until the onion has softened. Add the squash, almonds and stock and bring to the boil, then reduce the heat and simmer for 25 minutes, or until the squash is softened.

Transfer to a blender or use a hand-held stick blender to blitz to a smooth purée. Strain through a fine sieve.

Return to a clean pan, stir in the cream, then bring the soup back almost to boiling point.

Divide the soup between the individual soup bowls and sprinkle generously with crushed amaretti biscuits and Parmesan cheese. Serve immediately.

Variations: Butternut Squash with Chestnut Honey Whipped Cream Proceed as for the basic soup but replace the amaretti with 4 tbsp lightly whipped cream, sweetened with 1 tbsp chestnut honey or traditional honey and spooned over the surface of the soup before serving. Top with some savoury croûtons and chopped flat-leaf parsley.

Creamed Swede, Red Chilli and Maple Soup Proceed as for the basic soup but replace the squash with swede. When adding the swede, also add ½ small red chilli, deseeded and finely chopped. Add 1 tbsp good-quality maple syrup together with the cream.

The fennel in this soup helps to accentuate the flavour and enhance the sweetness of the chestnuts in quite a remarkable way. I created this recipe – as you do! – when I had chestnuts and fennel left over from garnishing a pheasant dish one Christmas. The soup was a great success and I now make it regularly in autumn and winter. It always garners many plaudits.

chestnut and fennel soup with sherry and goat's curd gougères

25g (scant 1oz/2 tbsp) unsalted butter

2 onions, coarsely chopped

1 celery stick, coarsely chopped

2 heads fresh fennel, trimmed and coarsely chopped

400g (14oz) vacuum-packed chestnuts or 450g (1lb) canned chestnut purée

1.5 litres (2¾ pints/1.3 quarts) brown chicken stock (see p.19) or game stock (see p.22)

1 tsp fennel seeds

2 tsp caster sugar

1 tbsp dry sherry (such as Amontillado)

sea salt and freshly ground black pepper

For the goat's curd cream

75ml (2½ fl oz/⅓ cup) double cream

100g (3½oz/½ cup) goat's cheese

To garnish

12 gougères (see p.12), filled with goat's curd cream (see recipe)

few sprigs of chervil

Heat the butter in a heavy-based pan, then add the onions, celery and fennel and cook for 15–20 minutes, or until softened. Add the chestnuts or chestnut purée and the stock, and bring to the boil. Add the fennel seeds and sugar, then reduce the heat and simmer for 20 minutes, or until softened.

Transfer to a blender or use a hand-held stick blender to blitz to a smooth purée. Strain through a fine sieve. Return to the heat, add the sherry and season to taste.

To make the goat's curd cream, whip the cream until it forms soft peaks, then add the goat's cheese and some freshly ground black pepper. Mix well. Cut the gougères in half horizontally, then carefully fill each one with some goat's curd cream.

Divide the soup between 4 individual soup bowls, put 3 gougères in the centre of each, garnish with some chervil and serve immediately.

Variation: Chestnut and Fennel Soup with Smoked Bacon

Proceed as for the basic soup but omit the gougères. Instead, serve the soup topped with 50g (1¾oz) crispy-fried diced smoked bacon mixed with 1 tbsp chopped flat-leaf parsley.

Mustard seeds, mustard-seed oil and curry leaves can be found in Indian grocers and at good supermarkets. If you can't find mustard-seed oil, it is fine to use all sunflower oil instead. To ring the changes, you can make this soup with all manner of vegetables. Try pumpkin, squash or sweet potato, for example.

carrot soup with seven spices

1 tbsp mustard-seed oil

1 tbsp sunflower oil

2½ tsp black mustard seeds

12 small curry leaves

1 onion, coarsely chopped

1 garlic clove, coarsely chopped

450g (1lb) carrots, cut into small chunks

2.5cm (1in) piece of root ginger, finely chopped

1 tbsp Madras curry powder

1 red chilli, deseeded and finely chopped

½ tsp cumin seeds

10 cardamom seeds, cracked and inner seeds removed

2 tbsp coarsely chopped coriander

1 litre (1¾ pints/4 cups) vegetable stock (see p.22)

pinch of ground turmeric

sea salt and freshly ground black pepper

75ml (2½fl oz/⅓ cup) thick Greek-style natural yoghurt

Heat the mustard-seed oil and the sunflower oil in a large pan, then add the mustard seeds and curry leaves and cook over a medium heat for about 15 seconds, stirring continuously until the mustard seeds begin to pop. Remove half the curry leaves and half the mustard seeds with a slotted spoon and set aside.

Add the onion, garlic, carrots, ginger, curry powder, chilli, cumin, cardamom and coriander to the pan, cover with a lid, reduce the heat and cook over a low heat for 15 minutes, or until the vegetables are softened.

Remove the lid, pour the stock over and bring to the boil. Add the turmeric and a little salt, reduce the heat and simmer for 20 minutes.

Transfer to a blender or use a hand-held stick blender to blitz to a smooth purée. Strain through a fine sieve.

Return the soup to a clean pan, bring back to the boil, then remove from the heat. Stir in the yoghurt and adjust the seasoning to taste.

Divide the soup between 4 individual soup bowls and scatter with the reserved fried curry leaves and mustard seeds. Serve immediately.

Variation: Carrot, Pineapple and Ginger Soup Proceed as for the basic soup, using the ginger but omitting the other spices. Pour 750ml (1¼ pints/3 cups) vegetable stock over and 250ml (9fl oz/1 cup) fresh or bought pineapple juice. Purée in a blender and season to taste. Omit the yoghurt. This soup is delicious either hot or cold.

THIS PAGE: Carrot Soup with Seven Spices (recipe page 92)

OPPOSITE: Courgette and Basil Soup with Prosciutto Tartines (recipe page 97)

This elegant soup is derived from a very humble vegetable – the courgette – and is infused with basil, one of my favourite herbs. The soup is finished with a little cream and unsalted butter to enrich it, while the simple-to-make tartines lift it to another level. I sometimes forgo the tartines and instead flavour the soup with some curry powder and a teaspoon of freshly grated ginger, added at the same time as the courgettes and lettuce. Both recipes are equally delicious.

courgette and basil soup with prosciutto tartines

25g (scant 1oz/2 tbsp) unsalted butter

1 onion, coarsely chopped

1 garlic clove, crushed

50g (1¾oz) floury potatoes, peeled and finely cubed

4 large courgettes, thinly sliced

1 small round butter lettuce, leaves removed and well washed

1 litre (1¾ pints/4 cups) hot white chicken stock (see p.17)

12 basil leaves, shredded, plus extra to garnish or 10g (¼oz) baby basil, chopped, plus extra, unchopped, to garnish

100ml (3½fl oz/scant ½ cup) double cream

sea salt and freshly ground black pepper

For the tartines

2 slices of white bread, crusts removed

2 tbsp extra virgin olive oil

100g (3½oz) sliced prosciutto (Parma ham)

Firstly make the tartines. Toast the bread on both sides then brush one side with a little oil. Top each slice with a layer of overlapping prosciutto, then cut into 1cm (½in) wide fingers. Set aside.

For the soup, heat half the butter in a heavy-based pan, then add the onion, garlic and potatoes. Cook over a gentle heat for 4–5 minutes, or until the vegetables are softened. Add the courgettes and lettuce and cook for 2–3 minutes more.

Add the hot stock and bring to the boil, then reduce the heat and simmer gently for no more than 5 minutes to preserve the fresh flavour. Add the basil leaves or baby basil and stir.

Transfer to a blender or use a hand-held stick blender to blitz to a smooth purée. If you want a smoother soup, strain it through a fine sieve.

Return the soup to a clean pan and bring it back to the boil. Add the cream, whisk in the remaining butter and season to taste.

Divide between 4 hot individual soup bowls, sprinkle with the extra basil leaves or with baby basil and serve with the tartines.

hearty and wholesome

Susan is a great friend. She is co-owner of Bayona, the New Orleans restaurant that opened in 1990. Susan has won numerous awards and received many accolades during her career and is recognised as one of America's leading female chefs of her generation. I had the pleasure of inviting Susan to cook with me here at The Lanesborough some years back for our guests in the restaurant. Her hearty, flavoursome gumbo – a dish that is traditional to Louisiana and to Susan's culinary roots – is a real winner.

SUSAN SPICER'S
roast duck, andouille and greens gumbo

4 small duck legs

2 tbsp unsalted butter

2 tbsp plain flour

1 large onion, coarsely chopped

1 red pepper, deseeded and cut into 1cm (½in) cubes

1 celery stick, coarsely chopped

175g (6oz) andouille sausage

1 x 400g (14oz) can chopped tomatoes in juice or 400g (14oz) fresh tomatoes

2 garlic cloves, crushed

1.2 litres (2 pints/5 cups) white chicken stock (see p.17)

1 tbsp sunflower oil

75g (2½oz) okra (fresh or frozen), sliced

2 tbsp white wine vinegar

175g (6oz) Swiss chard or mustard greens, coarsely chopped

3 spring onions, coarsely chopped

1 tsp thyme leaves

1 bouquet garni (parsley, thyme and 1 bayleaf)

1 tbsp Worcestershire sauce

sea salt and freshly ground black pepper

Tabasco sauce

To serve

2 spring onions, shredded

100g (3½oz/⅔ cup) cooked long-grain rice (optional)

Preheat the oven to 160°C (325°F/Gas 3). Put the duck legs in a roasting tin and place in the preheated oven. Roast for 50–60 minutes, or until cooked through and tender. Remove from the oven and leave to cool. When cool enough to handle, pick all the meat off the bones and set aside.

Heat the butter in a heavy-based pan over a medium-low heat, then whisk in the flour. Stir continuously over a low heat for 10–15 minutes, or until the roux turns a deep peanut-butter brown.

Add the onion, pepper and celery, increase the heat to medium and cook gently for 5 minutes, or until the vegetables begin to soften. Stir in the sausage and cook for 5 minutes more. Add the tomatoes and garlic, then whisk in the stock, a little at a time, until smooth. Set aside.

Heat the oil in a frying pan over a medium heat, then add the okra and cook for 5 minutes. Add the vinegar, cook for 30 seconds more, then add the contents of the frying pan to the soup pan.

Add the chard or mustard greens and the spring onions. Bring to the boil, reduce the heat and add the thyme, bouquet garni, Worcestershire sauce and a little salt. Simmer over a low heat for 1 hour, skimming off any impurities that float to the surface.

Add the duck meat and cook for 2 minutes more to heat the meat through. Remove the bouquet garni, adjust the seasoning and add a touch of Tabasco to taste.

Divide between 4 individual soup bowls, scatter with the spring onion garnish and top with the cooked rice, if using. Serve immediately.

Although this soup is rustic and chunky, you may prefer it smoother. If so, simply blend it in a liquidiser. Moong dal are easy to cook as they don't need prior soaking.

yellow dal and peanut soup with chopped peanuts and coriander

300g (10oz/1½ cups) moong dal (yellow split mung beans)

1 litre (1¾ pints/4 cups) vegetable stock (see p.22)

200ml (7fl oz/¾ cup) coconut milk

2 tbsp sunflower oil

½ tsp mustard seeds

6 fresh or frozen curry leaves

1 green chilli, deseeded and finely chopped

2 tsp tamarind paste

¼ tsp ground turmeric

1 tsp brown sugar

2 tbsp roasted peanuts

sea salt

To garnish

2 tbsp coarsely chopped coriander

2 tbsp coarsely chopped roasted peanuts

Put the moong dal in a large pan, cover with the stock and bring to the boil. Reduce the heat and simmer for 40–45 minutes, or until the moong dal are softened and slightly mushy. Add the coconut milk. The soup should be of a fairly thick but sloppy consistency.

Meanwhile, heat the oil in a small frying pan over a medium-low heat, then add the mustard seeds. When they begin to pop, add the curry leaves and chilli. Reduce the heat to low and fry gently for 20 seconds to allow the oil to become infused with the flavours.

Stir in the tamarind, turmeric, sugar and 100ml (3½fl oz/scant ½ cup) water. Bring to the boil. Add the peanuts and a little salt and simmer for 2 minutes. Add to the moong dal and stir to combine.

Divide between 4 individual soup bowls. Sprinkle over the garnish of chopped coriander and the coarsely chopped peanuts. Serve immediately.

COOK'S SECRET

When cooking pulses, never add salt to the water as this toughens the skin, which stops the pulses from cooking and makes them hard. Cooking times can vary: usually the older the pulses are, the longer they take to cook. If all the liquid is absorbed during cooking, you may need to add more.

This warming, filling soup captures all the flavours of Spain and is ideal as a supper dish, served with crusty bread. Traditional salt cod can be too salty so I often prefer to make my own lighter version, as here. I also sometimes like to top the soup with freshly shaved Manchego cheese.

salt cod, chickpea and chorizo soup

400g (14oz) cod fillet, skin removed and cut into 2cm (¾in) pieces

1 tbsp coarse sea salt

2 tbsp extra virgin olive oil

1 onion, coarsely chopped

2 garlic cloves, crushed

1 large carrot, coarsely chopped

200g (7oz) cooking chorizo sausage, skin removed and cut into 1cm (½in) slices

1 x 400g (14oz) can chickpeas, rinsed and drained

1 red pepper, deseeded and cut into 1cm (½in) cubes

¼ tsp smoked paprika (pimentón)

1.5 litres (2¾ pints/1.3 quarts) white chicken stock (see p.17)

good pinch of saffron strands

1 tsp finely chopped oregano or ½ tsp dried oregano

75g (2½oz) Serrano ham, coarsely chopped

125g (4½oz) baby spinach, leaves only, shredded

crusty bread, to serve

Put the cod in a dish, sprinkle with the salt and leave uncovered in the fridge for 1 hour.

Meanwhile, heat the oil in a large pan over a medium heat, then add the onion, garlic and carrot. Cook for 10 minutes until softened. Add the chorizo, chickpeas, red pepper and paprika, reduce the heat to low and cook for 10 minutes more. Add the stock, saffron and oregano and bring to the boil. Reduce the heat and simmer for 10 minutes.

Remove the cod from the fridge, rinse under a little cold water and pat dry with kitchen paper. Add the cod to the soup together with the Serrano ham and spinach. Simmer for 5 minutes more.

Divide the soup between individual soup bowls and serve immediately with plenty of crusty bread.

The combination of the pearl barley, spelt and lentils gives this soup a lovely real wintry feel. The smoked cheese adds an interesting smoky flavour that blends beautifully with the other ingredients.

farmhouse soup

2 tbsp extra virgin olive oil

300g (10oz) stewing beef (such as chuck or skirt), cut into 2cm (¾in) cubes

1 onion, coarsely chopped

2 garlic cloves, crushed

1 small bayleaf

2 sprigs of thyme

75g (2½oz/⅓ cup) pearl barley

75g (2½oz/⅓ cup) spelt

75g (2½oz/generous ⅓ cup) Puy lentils

150g (5½oz) marrow or courgettes, cut into 2cm (¾in) cubes

1 carrot, cut into 2cm (¾in) cubes

100g (3½oz) butternut squash, peeled and cut into 2cm (¾in) cubes

2 medium potatoes, peeled and cut into 2cm (¾in) cubes

sea salt and freshly ground black pepper

crusty bread, to serve

To garnish

2 tbsp coarsely chopped flat-leaf parsley

75g (2½oz/½ cup) finely grated smoked provolone cheese

Heat the oil in a large pan over a medium heat, then add the beef and fry, stirring occasionally, for about 10 minutes, or until golden. Remove with a slotted spoon and set aside.

Add the onion and garlic to the pan, reduce the heat to low and cook for about 10 minutes, or until softened.

Return the beef to the pan and add the bayleaf, thyme, barley, spelt and lentils. Add 1.5 litres (2¾ pints/1.3 quarts) water and bring to the boil.

Reduce the heat and simmer gently for 1 hour, or until the beef and grains are cooked through and tender. Skim off any impurities that float to the surface. Add the marrow or courgettes, carrot, squash and potatoes. Cook for 20 minutes more.

Season the soup to taste and divide between 4 individual soup bowls. Sprinkle over the parsley, top with the grated cheese and serve with plenty of crusty bread.

Ever since Columbus brought red pepper plants back from the New World, Europeans have been drying and grinding them into a bright red powder called paprika. Over the centuries paprika has become more refined and its heat has mellowed somewhat. This Hungarian goulash soup is topped with tiny light dumplings known as *knoephla* or *knöpfle*. The dumplings are cooked in water before being added to the soup.

goulash soup with knoephla

2 tbsp extra virgin olive oil

800g (1¾lb) stewing beef (such as chuck or skirt), fat removed and cut into 2.5cm (1in) cubes

1 large onion, finely chopped

2 garlic cloves, crushed

2 tbsp sweet Hungarian paprika

2 tsp caraway seeds

1 tbsp tomato purée

1 tbsp plain flour

1.5 litres (2¾ pints/1.3 quarts) beef stock (see p.22)

1 x 400g (14oz) can chopped tomatoes in juice

1 large carrot, cut into 1cm (½in) cubes

1 red pepper, deseeded and cut into 1cm (½in) cubes

1 medium potato, peeled and cut into 1cm (½in) cubes

sea salt and freshly ground black pepper

For the knoephla

150g (5½oz/1 cup) plain flour, plus extra for dusting

1 egg, lightly beaten

60ml (2fl oz/¼ cup) whole milk (or water)

2 tbsp coarsely chopped flat-leaf parsley

sea salt

Heat the oil in a pan over a medium heat, then add the beef and fry, stirring occasionally, for about 10 minutes, or until golden. Add the onion and garlic and cook for 5 minutes, or until the onions have softened.

Add the paprika and caraway seeds and cook for 2 minutes more, then add the tomato purée. Cook for 2 minutes, then sprinkle over the flour and cook for 2 minutes more.

Pour the stock over and bring to the boil. Add the tomatoes and their juice together with the carrot, red pepper and potato. Reduce the heat and simmer for 1½ hours, or until the beef is tender. If necessary, add a little more stock or water to the pan.

Meanwhile, prepare the knoephla. Combine all the ingredients in a bowl and mix well with a wooden spoon to form a stiff dough. Using floured hands, roll the dough out on a floured work surface into 2cm (¾in) 'ropes'.

Bring a large pan of water to the boil, then reduce the heat to a simmer. Using kitchen scissors, snip the dough into 1cm (½in) lengths straight into the simmering water. They will float to the surface.

Cook for 10 minutes, then carefully remove with a slotted spoon. Season the soup to taste, then divide between 4 individual soup bowls. Top each bowl with some of the knoepfla and serve immediately.

COOK'S SECRET

You could make this soup in a slow cooker, which would allow the meat to cook until it is meltingly tender.

Variation: Knoepfla Soup Knoepfla Soup is a German soup that is popular in the USA. This is my version. Follow the Potato and Leek Soup recipe on p.151. Make double the amount of knoepfla from the basic recipe and add to the potato and leek soup.

Over my years as a chef I've tasted many variations of borscht, both Russian and Polish at their best; all vary in flavour and ingredients. This recipe is adapted from one served some 15 years ago when I invited the chef from Moscow's Café Pushkin to cook with me at The Lanesborough. It is the best borscht I have tasted; the addition of a little thinly sliced smoked duck or goose breast adds a pleasant smokiness to the sweet-and-sour beetroot soup. For best results, I recommend you make this soup a day ahead to allow the flavours to mellow and blend.

borscht

400g (14oz) beef chuck, fat and sinew removed and cut into 2.5cm (1in) cubes

2 litres (3½ pints/8½ cups) beef stock (see p.22)

4 tbsp extra virgin olive oil

1 onion, coarsely chopped

½ tsp caraway seeds

2 carrots, grated

1 turnip, peeled and grated

1 parsnip, peeled and grated

1 small celeriac, peeled and grated

2 large garlic cloves, crushed

10 allspice berries

1 small bayleaf

2 tsp tomato purée

300g (10oz) raw beetroot, peeled and coarsely grated

¼ small white cabbage, cored, shredded

2 tbsp red wine vinegar

2 tbsp caster sugar

sea salt and freshly ground black pepper

200g (7oz) kielbasa sausage, thinly sliced

1 smoked duck or goose breast, skin removed and thinly sliced

2 tbsp coarsely chopped flat-leaf parsley

2 tbsp coarsely chopped dill

To serve

crusty bread

100ml (3½fl oz/scant ½ cup) sour cream

The day before, put the beef in a large pan, cover with water and bring to the boil. Reduce the heat and simmer for 5 minutes, then strain through a colander and rinse the meat under cold water.

Return the blanched beef to a clean pan, add the beef stock and bring to the boil. Reduce the heat and simmer for 1–1½ hours. Skim off any impurities that float to the surface.

Meanwhile, heat a large dry frying pan over a medium heat. When the pan is hot, add the oil, then the onion. Fry over a medium-low heat for 10 minutes, or until the onion is softened and slightly coloured.

Add the caraway seeds, carrots, turnip, parsnip, celeriac, garlic, allspice and bayleaf, cover with a lid and cook for 10 minutes more until the vegetables begin to soften. Add the tomato purée and cook for 5 minutes more.

Transfer the contents of the frying pan to the beef pan and add the beetroot and cabbage. Simmer for 15–20 minutes, or until all the vegetables are tender. Add the vinegar, sugar, a little salt and the sausage and duck breast. Simmer for 10 minutes more to heat the sausage and duck through.

Remove the allspice and bayleaf from the pan, then add half the parsley and half the dill and adjust the seasoning. The flavour should be a nice balance between sweetness and acidity, in other words, neither too sour nor too sweet. Remove the pan from the heat, cool, then chill overnight to allow the flavours to develop.

The next day, bring the soup back to the boil and continue heating it for 2–3 minutes to ensure it is very hot. Divide between the individual soup bowls and top with the remaining chopped parsley and dill. Serve with plenty of crusty bread and with the sour cream.

This is one of the many great soups of Italian cookery, and there is no finer Italian cook than my friend Antonio Carluccio to tell us the secret of the perfect pasta and bean soup. It is best to use fresh borlotti beans, which are occasionally found outside Italy. Available around August and September, they are recognisable by the green and red colouring of their pods. If you can't find them, you can substitute canned or dried beans, or use white cannellini beans instead.

ANTONIO CARLUCCIO'S
pasta e fagioli

1kg (2¼lb) fresh borlotti beans or 2 x 400g (14oz) cans of borlotti or cannellini beans or 250g (9oz/ 1½ cups) dried borlotti beans

4 tbsp extra virgin olive oil, plus extra to serve

2 celery sticks, finely chopped

115g (4oz) prosciutto (Parma ham) trimmings, chopped into small cubes

2 medium potatoes, peeled and cubed

1 fresh red chilli, coarsely chopped

2 garlic cloves, finely chopped

3 ripe tomatoes, blanched, peeled and chopped or 1 x 400g (14oz) can chopped tomatoes in juice

1 litre (1¾ pints/4 cups) white chicken stock (see p.17) or beef stock (see p.22) or water

115g (4oz) tubettini or other small pasta

10 fresh basil leaves, shredded

sea salt and freshly ground black pepper

If you are using dried beans, prepare them the day before by leaving them to soak in water overnight. The next day, drain, then boil the beans in unsalted water for 2–3 hours, or until tender. Drain.

If using fresh beans, boil in unsalted water for 30–40 minutes, or until cooked, then drain. If using canned beans, simply drain, rinse and drain again.

Heat the oil over a medium heat in a large saucepan. Add the celery and prosciutto and fry for a couple of minutes. Add the potatoes and chilli, stirring well to prevent the ham from browning. Cook for about 10 minutes, then add the garlic and cook for a couple of minutes more.

Add the tomatoes and cook for 10 minutes more.

Add two-thirds of the drained beans. Mash the remainder and set aside.

Pour the stock or water over the mixture in the pan and bring to the boil. Add the pasta, reduce the heat and cook for 8 minutes, or until the pasta is al dente. Add the basil and the mashed beans and season to taste with salt and pepper.

Just before serving, add a drizzle of olive oil to each bowl. This will enhance the flavour amazingly.

THIS PAGE: Italian Wedding Soup
(recipe page 117)

OPPOSITE: Tuscan White Bean Soup
with Tuna Bottarga (recipe page 116)

Bottarga is salted pressed tuna roe (it can also be made from mullet roe) and is one of the gastronomic delicacies of Italy. It is sometimes referred to as Sicilian caviar and, like its namesake, it is relatively expensive. Here it is shaved thinly, so a little goes a long way. You can buy it from good Italian delis.

tuscan white bean soup with tuna bottarga

300g (10oz/1¾ cups) white beans, soaked overnight, drained

1 onion, coarsely chopped

3 garlic cloves, crushed

1 small bayleaf

1 sprig of rosemary

750ml (1¼ pints/3 cups) white chicken stock (see p.17) or vegetable stock (see p.22)

200ml (7fl oz/¾ cup) whole milk

sea salt and freshly ground black pepper

75ml (2½fl oz/⅓ cup) extra virgin olive oil

150g (5½oz) tuna bottarga, very thinly shaved

Put the drained beans in a large pan, add the onion, half the garlic, the bayleaf and rosemary. Pour 1 litre (1¾ pints/4 cups) water over, then bring to the boil. Reduce the heat and simmer for 1 hour, or until the beans are tender. Drain the beans, reserving 400ml (14fl oz/1¾ cups) of the cooking liquid.

Put the cooked beans in a clean pan with the reserved cooking liquid, the stock and the milk. Bring to the boil, then reduce the heat and simmer for 25 minutes. Remove the bayleaf and rosemary.

Transfer to a blender or use a hand-held stick blender to blitz until smooth. Season to taste and set aside.

Heat the oil in a small pan over a medium heat, then add the remaining garlic and reduce the heat to the lowest possible. Cook for 1 minute to infuse the oil with the garlic, making sure that the garlic doesn't colour.

Whisk half the garlic oil into the soup then divide the soup between the individual soup bowls. Top with thin shavings of tuna bottarga, drizzle over the remaining garlic oil and serve immediately.

Variation: White Bean Soup with Rosemary Pistou Proceed as for the basic soup but replace the tuna with a good spoonful of rosemary pesto drizzled over each bowl. To make the pesto, simply add 2 tsp coarsely chopped rosemary to the basic pesto recipe (see p.163).

The origins of this soup's name are a little mysterious. Some cooks say it is traditionally served at Italian weddings, while others say the name comes from the way the ingredients marry so well together. Whatever the truth of the matter, this soup really is a marriage of great ingredients and it's also extremely hearty and nutritious. You can replace the lettuce with other greens – kale, chard or even spinach if you like.

italian wedding soup

3 tbsp extra virgin olive oil

1 onion, finely chopped

1 garlic clove, crushed

½ tsp red chilli flakes

1.5 litres (2¾ pints/1.3 quarts) white chicken stock (see p.17)

75g (2½oz) orzo or tubettini pasta

300g (10oz) escarole lettuce, coarsely chopped

2 tbsp coarsely chopped flat-leaf parsley

1 egg

150g (5½oz/1⅓ cups) freshly grated Pecorino Romano

sea salt and freshly ground black pepper

For the meatballs

200g (7oz/1⅔ cups) minced beef

200g (7oz/1⅔ cups) minced pork

grated zest of ¼ lemon

1 egg

100g (3½oz/scant 1 cup) freshly grated Pecorino Romano

1 tbsp coarsely chopped fresh oregano or ½ tsp dried oregano

Firstly make the meatballs. Combine all the ingredients together in a bowl, season to taste, then refrigerate for 1 hour. Remove from the fridge and, using wet hands, roll the meat mixture into 2.5cm (1in) diameter balls.

Heat a large frying pan with 2 tbsp of the oil over a medium-low heat, then add the meatballs and cook for 5–8 minutes, or until golden all over. Remove with a slotted spoon onto kitchen paper to drain. Set aside.

For the soup, heat the remaining oil in a clean pan over a medium heat and add the onion, garlic and chilli flakes. Reduce the heat to low and cook for 10 minutes, or until the onion is softened.

Pour the stock over, bring to the boil, then reduce the heat to a simmer. Add the pasta and lettuce and simmer for 10–12 minutes, or until the pasta is al dente. Add the meatballs to the broth and simmer for 5 minutes more. Add the parsley.

Meanwhile, whisk together the egg and Pecorino Romano in a bowl. Slowly pour the egg and Pecorino Romano mixture into the soup, stirring continuously and always in the same direction with a wooden spoon as you pour.

Simmer for 30 seconds over the lowest heat to allow the eggs to cook and thicken slightly. Season to taste. Divide the soup between individual soup bowls and serve immediately.

Harissa is a heavy, spicy condiment used extensively in Moroccan and Tunisian cooking. Though traditionally made with a base of fiery red chilli, here I use green chillies which are equally delicious. Use any leftover harissa to toss through pasta.

moroccan vegetable soup with green harissa and couscous

300g (10oz/1¾ cups) dried chickpeas, soaked overnight, drained (see Cook's secret)

1 onion, coarsely chopped

1 small bayleaf

2 tsp ground cumin

2 tbsp extra virgin olive oil

2 garlic cloves, crushed

2 turnips, peeled and cut into 1cm (½in) cubes

2 carrots, cut into 1cm (½in) cubes

1 sweet potato, peeled and cut into 1cm (½in) cubes

1 red pepper, halved, deseeded and cut into 1cm (½in) cubes

1 tsp paprika

¼ tsp red chilli flakes

¼ tsp ground turmeric

2cm (¾in) piece of root ginger, finely chopped

1 litre (1¾ pints/4 cups) vegetable stock (see p.22)

1 x 400g (14oz) can chopped tomatoes in juice

75g (2½oz/generous ⅓ cup) couscous

2 tbsp coarsely chopped mint

1 tbsp coarsely chopped coriander

2 tbsp fresh lemon juice

For the green harissa

50g (1¾oz/1 cup) fresh coriander, coarsely chopped

3 tbsp extra virgin olive oil

1 garlic clove, crushed

1 green chilli, deseeded and finely chopped

¼ tsp ground cumin

½ tsp ground ginger

sea salt

Put the chickpeas in a pan, add 1.5 litres (2¾ pints/1.3 quarts) water, half the onion, the bayleaf and half the cumin. Bring to the boil, then reduce the heat and simmer for 1–1¼ hours, or until the chickpeas are tender. Drain and set aside. Discard the bayleaf.

Heat the oil in another pan over a medium heat, then add the remaining onion, the garlic, turnips, carrots, sweet potato and red pepper, together with the paprika, chilli flakes, turmeric and root ginger. Reduce the heat to low, cover with a lid and cook for 5 minutes, or until the vegetables begin to soften. Add the cooked chickpeas and stir.

Pour the stock over, add the tomatoes and bring to the boil. Reduce the heat and simmer for 20 minutes, until the flavours are well blended.

Meanwhile, prepare the green harissa. Place all the ingredients in a small blender and blitz to a coarse purée.

Ten minutes or so before you are ready to serve, put the couscous in a bowl, pour 150ml (5fl oz/⅔ cup) boiling water over and cover with clingfilm. Leave to stand for 5 minutes, then remove the clingfilm. Fluff up the couscous with a fork, cover again with clingfilm and leave to stand for 5 minutes more.

To finish the soup, add the mint, coriander and lemon juice, then stir in 3 tbsp of the green harissa. Cook for 2 minutes, then divide the soup between the individual soup bowls and serve immediately, topped with a scattering of steamed couscous.

COOK'S SECRET

In the Middle East many cooks add a little bicarbonate of soda to the water in which the chickpeas are soaked, plus a little more to the chickpeas as they cook. The bicarbonate of soda helps to make the chickpeas more digestible.

Here is my recipe for this classic Caribbean soup; it's extremely hearty and packed with excitement. Traditionally made with yams – not one of my favourite vegetables as I find them quite starchy – here I use squash. Heresy, I hear you say, but I think the squash adds some sweetness to the overall flavour. I also use spinach instead of callaloo, which can be difficult to find unless you have a Caribbean grocer or market nearby.

jamaican pepper pot soup

2 tbsp sunflower oil

400g (14oz) salt beef, cut into 1cm (½in) cubes

200g (7oz) bacon rashers, finely chopped

1 litre (1¾ pints/4 cups) beef stock (see p.22) or water

2 sprigs of thyme

1 small red pepper, deseeded and coarsely chopped

1 small green pepper, deseeded and coarsely chopped

½ small Scotch bonnet chilli pepper, deseeded and finely chopped

½ small butternut squash, peeled and cut into small cubes

100g (3½oz) okra (fresh or frozen)

1 x 400g (14oz) can coconut milk

300g (10oz) fresh callaloo or fresh spinach, finely shredded

2 spring onions, finely shredded

sea salt and freshly ground black pepper

2 tbsp white wine vinegar

Heat the oil in a heavy-based pan over a medium heat, then add the beef and fry for 10 minutes, or until lightly golden. Remove from the pan with a slotted spoon.

Add the bacon to the pan and fry for 2–3 minutes, or until golden. Return the beef to the pan, cover with the stock or water and add the thyme. Reduce the heat and simmer for 1 hour, skimming off any impurities that float to the surface.

Add the red and green peppers, chilli, squash, okra and coconut milk. Simmer for 15 minutes more, then add the callaloo or spinach and the spring onion. Cook for 15 minutes more, or until the beef is beautifully tender and the soup slightly thickened.

Season to taste and stir in the vinegar. Divide the soup between individual soup bowls and serve immediately.

This staple French soup is traditionally served in bistros and brasseries throughout France and worldwide. But there is nothing standard about it. It is the perfect example of how the simplest, most basic of ingredients can produce something really special. This recipe comes courtesy of great chefs and friends, brothers Chris and Jeff Galvin, who, in my opinion, have revolutionised and reinvented bistro cooking in Britain. Chris says that for the best results, you will need to start with a full-bodied stock.

CHRIS AND JEFF GALVIN'S
soupe a l'oignon gratinée

50g (1¾oz/3½ tbsp) unsalted butter

4 large onions, finely sliced

1 tbsp thyme leaves

1 bayleaf

2 garlic cloves, sliced

75ml (2½fl oz/⅓ cup) white wine

3 litres (5¼ pints/2.6 quarts or 12 cups) brown chicken stock (see p.19)

120ml (4fl oz/½ cup) white port

sea salt and freshly ground white pepper

125g (4½oz/1 cup) Gruyère cheese, grated

For the croûtons

¼ French baguette

extra virgin olive oil, for drizzling

Melt the butter in a heavy-based saucepan, then add the onions and cook over a medium heat for 45 minutes, stirring occasionally until the onions are soft, caramelised and golden.

Add the thyme, bayleaf and garlic and cook for 10 minutes. Add the wine, bring to the boil and continue to boil until the wine is reduced by half. Pour in the stock, bring back to the boil, then reduce the heat and simmer gently for 1 hour.

Meanwhile, make the croûtons. Preheat the oven to 180°C (350°F/Gas 4). Cut the baguette into 3mm (⅛in) slices, put on a baking tray, then drizzle with the oil. Bake in the preheated oven for 7 minutes, or until golden. Set aside. Preheat the grill.

Stir the port into the soup and bring it back to the boil. Season to taste.

Divide the soup between 4 individual soup bowls and sprinkle each portion with the croûtons. Scatter with the Gruyère cheese, then put under a hot grill until the cheese colours and bubbles. Leave to cool for a couple of minutes before serving.

COOK'S SECRET

Chris and Jeff say the secret of this great classic onion soup is to caramelise the onions slowly to build up a good depth of colour.

Variation: Beer Soup Proceed as for the basic soup but replace the port with 275ml (9fl oz) bottle of dark beer and replace the Gruyère with a washed-rind cheese such as Vacherin or Livarot. This variation is typical of countries such as Switzerland and Germany.

THIS PAGE: Persian Red Lentil Soup
(recipe page 126)

OPPOSITE: Carrot, Tortilla and
Smoked Chilli Soup (recipe page 127)

There are many varieties of lentil-based soups in the cuisine of the Middle East, and especially in Egypt, Lebanon, Syria and Jordan. This is a classic soup that uses a little Middle-Eastern spice magic in the shape of baharat spices, also known as Arabic seven spices. Purists can buy it ready-made from Middle Eastern grocers. I include my recipe in the Cook's Secret.

persian red lentil soup

50g (1¾oz/3½ tbsp) unsalted butter

1 onion, coarsely chopped

200g (7oz/1 cup) red lentils, soaked overnight then drained

1 tsp ground cumin

1 tbsp baharat spices (see Cook's secret)

1.5 litres (2¾ pints/1.3 quarts) beef stock (see p.22)

sea salt and freshly ground black pepper

2 tbsp extra virgin olive oil

3 tbsp lemon juice

½ tsp dried mint

For the croûtons

4 slices crusty white bread, crusts removed and cut into 2cm (¾in) cubes

1 garlic clove, crushed

Heat half the butter in a large pan over a medium heat, then add the onion. Cook for 10 minutes until softened. Add the lentils, cumin and baharat spices. Mix together well and cook for 2 minutes. Pour the stock over and cook for 40 minutes, or until the lentils are tender.

Transfer to a blender or use a hand-held stick blender to blitz to a coarse purée. Season to taste and return to a clean pan.

For the croûtons, heat the remaining butter in a frying pan over a medium heat, then add the bread and the garlic. Fry for 1–2 minutes until golden and crispy.

Bring the soup to the boil. Stir in the oil, lemon juice and mint. Divide the soup between 4 individual soup bowls, top with the croûtons and serve immediately.

COOK'S SECRET

To make the baharat spices, mix together in a bowl: 2 tbsp black pepper, 2 tbsp paprika, 2 tbsp ground cumin, 2 tbsp ground coriander, 1 tsp ground cloves, 1 tsp ground cinnamon and 1 tsp ground cardamom. Store in a sealed container or jar until needed. This spice mix will keep fresh and aromatic for 1 month or more.

Variations: Lentil, Tomato and Cinnamon Soup Proceed as for the basic soup but replace the cumin with ground cinnamon and add 200ml (7fl oz/¾ cup) tomato passata or juice and 50g (1¾oz/⅓ cup) cooked basmati rice. Serve sprinkled with 2 tbsp coarsely chopped flat-leaf parsley.

Lentil Soup with Smoked Bacon, Feta and Za'atar Crisps Proceed as for the basic soup but add 100g (3½oz) crispy-fried cubed, smoked bacon 10 minutes before the soup is finished cooking. To serve, add 75g (2½oz/½ cup) crumbled feta cheese and top with za'atar spiced pitta bread crisps (see p.11).

This soup is a version of my good friend Dean Fearing's Tortilla Soup, a soup that Dean created many years ago while chef at the famous Mansion on Turtle Creek in Dallas USA. I have tweaked it slightly, but its essence remains the same – a great soup, packed with flavour and just the job on a cold winter's night. Chipotle chillies are dried Mexican chillies. They are dark in colour, smoky in flavour and worth looking out for. Corn tortillas are thin, unleavened Mexican flatbreads made from ground maize, which can be white, yellow or blue. I have only ever seen yellow maize here; it is available from good delis. Don't get corn tortillas confused with flour tortillas; those are entirely different and won't work in this wonderful soup.

carrot, tortilla and smoked chilli soup

2 tbsp sunflower oil

2 garlic cloves, crushed

2 large onions, coarsely grated

4 large carrots, coarsely chopped

handful of fresh coriander leaves

4 corn tortillas, cut into small pieces

1 small chipotle chilli, finely chopped (optional)

1 tbsp tomato purée

2 tsp ground cumin

1 tsp chilli powder

1 tsp smoked paprika

1 litre (1¾ pints/4 cups) white chicken stock (see p.17)

sea salt and freshly ground black pepper

To garnish

1 cooked chicken breast, finely shredded

½ avocado, peeled and cut into small cubes

75g (2½oz/⅔ cup) grated Cheddar cheese

2 corn tortillas, finely shredded and deep-fried until crispy

10g (¼oz) coriander micro cress

Heat the oil in a heavy-based pan over a medium heat, then add the garlic and onions and fry for 10 minutes, or until they begin to soften. Add the carrots and coriander and cook for 2–3 minutes.

Add the tortilla, the chipotle chilli, if using, the tomato purée and the cumin, chilli and paprika. Mix well and cook for 1 minute.

Pour the stock over and bring to the boil, then reduce the heat and simmer for 30 minutes, or until the carrots have softened. Transfer to a blender or use a hand-held stick blender to blitz to a smooth purée.

Season to taste. Divide the soup between 4 individual soup bowls and serve immediately, topped with the garnishes.

Sardines are tasty, nutritious and inexpensive, and are often neglected in Britain, though they are popular in countries such as Spain, Italy and Greece. I use them here to create a wonderful French bouillabaisse-style soup. I often like to accompany it with some toasted French bread croûtons, smeared with a little paprika-flavoured mayonnaise. If you are not sure about preparing the sardines, your fishmonger will be happy to do it for you.

sardine bouillabaisse

2 tbsp extra virgin olive oil

2 onions, coarsely chopped

1 garlic clove, crushed

2 small leeks, trimmed and cut into 2cm (¾in) slices

1 head fennel, trimmed and cut into 2cm (¾in) cubes

1 red pepper, deseeded and cut into 2cm (¾in) cubes

¼ tsp red chilli flakes

2 tbsp tomato purée

750ml (1¼ pints/3 cups) fish stock (see p.24)

1 small bayleaf

1 x 200g (7oz) can chopped tomatoes in juice

pinch of saffron strands

1 large potato, peeled and cut into 2cm (¾in) cubes

8 large sardines

3 tbsp anis liqueur (such as Pernod or Ricard)

sea salt and freshly ground black pepper

Heat the oil in a pan over a medium heat, then add the onions, garlic, leeks, fennel, red pepper and chilli flakes. Reduce the heat and cook over a low heat for 10 minutes, or until softened.

Add the tomato purée, stock, bayleaf, tomatoes, saffron and potato. Simmer for 20 minutes, or until the potato is cooked.

Meanwhile, clean the sardines. Cut off their heads, scale them, remove their spines and cut into 5cm (2in) pieces. Wash under running water and dry thoroughly in a cloth.

When the potato is cooked, carefully add the sardines and cook gently over a low heat for 3 minutes. Add the liqueur and adjust the seasoning. Divide the soup between 4 individual soup bowls and serve immediately.

Variation: Zuppa di Pesce Proceed as for the basic soup but add 1 tsp finely chopped oregano together with the tomatoes to make an Italian-style fish soup. Also, replace the sardines with 800g (1¾lb) mixed fish and shellfish of your choice, such as monkfish, red mullet, mussels, clams, etc.

Any type of sausage works for this soup: I like to use a mixture of smoked and fresh. The choice is yours. Available from September to March, curly kale is a hearty winter brassica with frilly leaves that have thick central veins. Make sure you buy your kale fresh and crisp.

sausage and curly kale chowder

1 tbsp extra virgin olive oil

300g (10oz) chicken sausages

100g (3½oz) cooking chorizo sausage, skinned and cut into 1cm (½in) slices

150g (5½oz) Kielbasa sausages, cut into 1cm (½in) slices

1 onion, coarsely chopped

2 garlic cloves, crushed

2 carrots, cut into 1cm (½in) cubes

2 celery sticks, cut into 1cm (½in) cubes

750ml (1¼ pints/3 cups) white chicken stock (see p.17)

2 sprigs of thyme

250g (9oz) new potatoes, peeled and cut into chunks

300g (10oz) curly kale, torn into small pieces

100ml (3½fl oz/scant ½ cup) single cream

sea salt and freshly ground black pepper

pinch of chilli powder

Heat the oil in a large pan over a medium heat, then add the chicken sausages. Reduce the heat and cook for 10–15 minutes, turning occasionally, until the sausages are cooked through. Remove from the pan with a slotted spoon and set aside. When cool enough to handle, cut into 2cm (¾in) slices.

Meanwhile, add the chorizo and Kielbasa sausage slices to the pan and fry for 2 minutes, turning occasionally, until lightly coloured. Remove from the pan with a slotted spoon and set aside.

Add the onion, garlic, carrots and celery to the juices in the pan, cover with a lid and cook for 5 minutes, or until the vegetables begin to soften. Pour the stock over and add the thyme and potatoes. Stir, then cover the pan and simmer for about 15 minutes, or until the vegetables are just tender.

Add the kale and simmer for 10–15 minutes, or until the kale is cooked. Add the cream, return all the sausages to the pan and season with salt, pepper and chilli powder to taste. Discard the thyme.

Divide the soup between 4 individual soup bowls and serve immediately.

Variation: Sausage and Mixed Bean Soup Proceed as for the basic soup but replace the chard with a can of drained and rinsed mixed beans. Omit the cream.

Cracked wheat, or bulghur, is a staple grain of Middle-Eastern cuisine, where it features in the famous tabbouleh salad. Here, made into wheat dumplings and added to a tasty roasted squash and lentil soup, it plays a much heartier role. This is my version of the traditional Lebanese 'monk's soup'.

cumin roasted squash and lentil soup with cracked wheat dumplings

1 tsp cumin seeds, toasted

1 medium butternut squash (about 400g/14oz), peeled and cut into 2.5cm (1in) cubes

4 tbsp extra virgin olive oil

sea salt and freshly ground black pepper

350g (12oz/1¾ cups) Puy lentils

1.2 litres (2 pints/5 cups) brown chicken stock (see p.19)

250g (9oz) baby spinach, washed and stalks removed

50g (1¾oz/⅓ cup) pine nuts, toasted

juice and grated zest of ½ lemon

For the dumplings

75g (2½oz/⅓ cup) fine cracked wheat (bulghur)

1 small onion, finely chopped

1 tbsp coarsely chopped mint

1 tbsp coarsely chopped coriander

1 tbsp coarsely chopped flat-leaf parsley

75g (2½oz/½ cup) plain flour, sieved

30g (1oz/⅓ cup) shredded vegetable suet

Preheat the oven to 220°C (425°F/Gas 7). Grind the cumin seeds in a spice or coffee grinder. Put the cubes of squash in a roasting tin, drizzle with 2 tbsp of the oil and season with salt, a little pepper and the ground cumin. Put in the preheated oven and roast for 25–30 minutes, or until the squash is a nice golden colour.

Remove half the squash from the tin and transfer to a clean pan. Set aside the remaining squash.

Add the lentils and 750ml (1¼ pints/3 cups) of the stock to the squash in the pan, bring to the boil, then reduce the heat and simmer for 40 minutes, or until just cooked.

Meanwhile, prepare the dumplings. Mix all the ingredients together in a bowl and add about 4 tbsp water to achieve a soft dough-like consistency. Season with salt and pepper.

Transfer the dough to a floured work surface, then take small amounts and roll in the palm of your hand to form small balls.

Bring the remaining stock to the boil in a pan, then reduce the heat to a simmer. Drop the dumplings into the simmering stock. Poach gently for 15–20 minutes until firm, then remove with a slotted spoon onto a dish. You may need to do this in batches.

Transfer a quarter of the squash and lentil soup to a blender or use a hand-held stick blender to blitz to a smooth purée. Return the purée to the rest of the squash and lentil soup, adding a little more stock if necessary. The soup should be slightly thick and pulpy in consistency.

Stir in the spinach, pine nuts, lemon juice and zest and adjust the seasoning. Return the dumplings to the soup. Divide between 4 individual soup bowls and serve immediately.

Variation: Squash and Butter Bean Soup Proceed as for the basic soup but replace the lentils with 1 x 400g (14oz) can drained and rinsed butter beans. Blitz to a purée to serve.

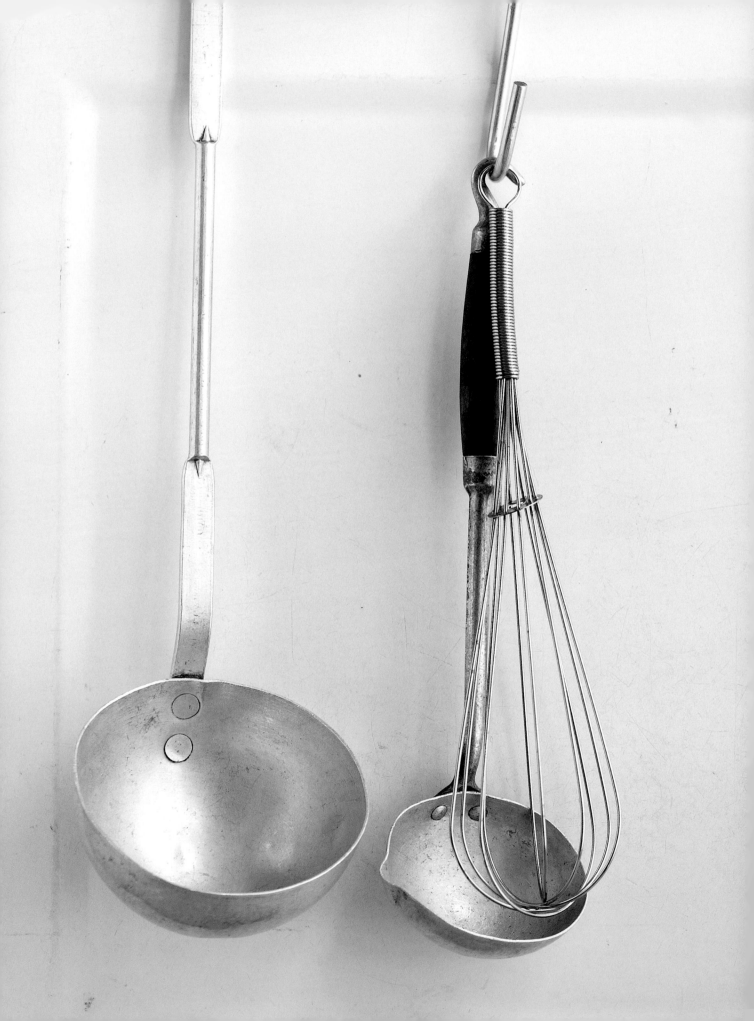

traditional favourites

Black beans are the staple food of southern Mexican and Brazilian cookery. They are full of nutrients and antioxidants. This smoky-tasting black bean soup originates from the Veracruz region of Mexico and is one I often prepare as I am a great lover of Mexico's wonderful food. The salsa sofrito adds a lively kick, while the sour cream or crème fraîche mellows the taste of the salsa. All in all, I'm sure you will enjoy preparing and eating this traditional favourite.

black bean soup with salsa sofrito

2 tbsp extra virgin olive oil

2 onions, coarsely chopped

2 garlic cloves, cut in half

1 tsp oregano leaves

375g (13oz/2⅛ cups) dried black beans, picked over and rinsed, but not soaked

1 x 400g (14oz) can chopped tomatoes in juice

1 tsp red chilli flakes

2 tsp cumin seeds, lightly toasted

½ tsp coriander seeds, toasted

1 tsp smoked paprika

juice of ¼ lemon

sea salt and freshly ground black pepper

100ml (3½fl oz/scant ½ cup) sour cream or crème fraîche, to serve

wedges of lime, to serve

For the salsa sofrito

2 tbsp canned chipotle chilli peppers in adobo sauce, coarsely chopped

2 firm ripe tomatoes, coarsely chopped

2 tbsp coarsely chopped coriander

1 small red onion, coarsely chopped

1 garlic clove, crushed

Firstly make the salsa sofrito. This can be made the day before if wished. Put all the ingredients in a bowl, mix well and leave to stand for 1 hour to allow the flavours to develop. Transfer to the fridge to chill.

For the soup, heat half the oil in a large heavy-based pan over a low heat. Add half the onion, half the garlic and the oregano and cook for 10 minutes, or until softened.

Add the beans and 1.5 litres (2¾ pints/1.3 quarts) water and bring to the boil. Discard any beans that float to the surface. Reduce the heat, cover the pan and simmer for 1½–2 hours, or until the beans are very tender.

Meanwhile, put the remaining onion and garlic, together with the tomatoes, chilli flakes, cumin, coriander and paprika in a blender. Blitz until smooth.

Heat the remaining oil in a frying pan, then add the contents of the blender. Cook for 15–20 minutes, or until the mix has reduced and is pulpy in consistency. Add to the beans, stir well and simmer for 15 minutes more.

Transfer to a blender or use a hand-held stick blender to blitz coarsely or to a smoother consistency if you prefer. Stir in the lemon juice and season to taste.

Divide the soup between 4 individual soup bowls and serve immediately with the sour cream or crème fraîche, the salsa sofrito and wedges of lime.

COOK'S SECRET

For a very much more rustic-style soup, simply serve the soup unblended but garnish with the salsa as for the basic soup.

Variation: Proceed as for the basic soup but add some sliced, sautéed merguez sausage or sliced chorizo sausages before serving.

This smooth, creamy, rich potato bisque is intensely ocean-flavoured, packed full of briny-tasting clams and with just a hint of onions. Serve piping hot with crusty bread for a real seafood-lover's treat. Traditionally made with large clams such as the American cherrystone variety, I prefer to use small ones. Some New England chowders contain tomatoes; this has been so controversial that a Bill was passed in New England in 1939, banning them from being added to this classic American soup. In a break with tradition and because I love their spiciness, I sprinkle over a few red chilli flakes before serving.

new england clam chowder

1.5kg (3lb 3oz) fresh clams (preferably vongole clams)

3 rashers of streaky bacon, finely chopped

50g (1¾oz/3½ tbsp) unsalted butter

2 large onions, coarsely chopped

½ tsp thyme leaves

1 bayleaf

50g (1¾oz/⅓ cup) plain flour

200ml (7fl oz/¾ cup) whole milk

4 large potatoes, peeled and cut into 2cm (¾in) cubes

150ml (5fl oz/⅔ cup) double cream

sea salt and freshly ground black pepper

red chilli flakes, to serve

Rinse the clams in a colander under cold water, then drain well, discarding any broken clams. Put in a large pan, cover with 1.5 litres (2¾ pints/ 1.3 quarts) water and bring to the boil.

When the clams open, after about 1 minute, drain, reserving the cooking liquid. Discard any clams that have remained unopened. Remove the clams from their shells, discard the shells and set the clams aside.

Cook the bacon in a dry pan over a medium heat for 2–3 minutes, or until crisp. Add the butter, onions, thyme and bayleaf. Reduce the heat and cook gently for 10 minutes, or until the onions are softened.

Add the flour and stir with a wooden spoon to make a roux around the onion and bacon mixture. Cook, stirring continuously for about 1 minute, or until the flour is cooked.

Add the clam cooking liquid and the milk. Bring to the boil. Reduce the heat and add the potatoes. Cook for 10 minutes, or until the potatoes are just tender. Add the cream and cook for 5 minutes more.

Return the clams to the soup and season to taste. Divide the soup between individual soup bowls, sprinkle with a few red chilli flakes and serve immediately.

Variation: Smoked Fish Chowder This simple version uses smoked fish, which is delicious. Proceed as for the basic soup but omit the clams. Cook the bacon, onions and thyme as before and make a roux. Instead of using the clam cooking liquid, add the same volume of fish stock (see p.24) together with the potatoes. When you add the cream, also add 200g (7oz) flaked smoked fish, such as salmon, trout, mackerel or eel. Stir in a little coarsely chopped flat-leaf parsley and serve. This is equally delicious made with white fish, such as cod, haddock or monkfish.

There are many stories as to the origin of the name of this mussel soup from Brittany. The most plausible is that it was created by the chef at Maxims in Paris for an American tin tycoon, William B Leeds, who adored both the taste of mussels and this soup. It is certainly one of my favourite ways to enjoy these delicious molluscs.

potage billi bi

1kg (2¼lb) fresh mussels in their shells

200ml (7fl oz/¾ cup) dry white wine

750ml (1¼ pints/3 cups) fish stock (see p.24)

2 shallots, finely chopped

sprig of thyme

1 bayleaf

1 tsp fresh saffron strands

25g (scant 1 oz/2 tbsp) unsalted butter

50g (1¾oz/⅓ cup) plain flour

200ml (7fl oz/¾ cup) double cream

1 egg yolk

sea salt and freshly ground black pepper

pinch of cayenne pepper

juice of ¼ lemon

Wash the mussels carefully, removing any sand and beards. Discard any mussels that are open as they are dead.

Put the wine, stock, shallots, thyme, bayleaf and saffron in a pan over a medium heat and bring to the boil. Add the mussels, cover with a tight-fitting lid, increase the heat to high and cook for 4–5 minutes, or until the mussels have opened.

Strain and reserve the cooking liquid and mussels separately. Discard any mussels that have not opened as these are dead, too.

Melt the butter in a clean pan over a low heat. Add the flour and stir with a wooden spoon to make a roux. Cook, stirring continuously for 2 minutes, or until the flour is cooked.

Add the strained cooking liquid, whisking continuously until the mixture is smooth and creamy. Simmer for 20 minutes, then add 100ml (3½fl oz/ scant ½ cup) of the cream. Cook for 10 minutes.

Meanwhile, shuck the mussels (remove from their shells) and remove any remaining beards.

Beat the egg and remaining cream together in a large bowl, then add a ladleful of the fish soup, whisking briskly and constantly. Return to the pan containing the rest of the soup. Stir over a low heat until almost boiling but do not let it boil.

Add the cleaned mussels and season with salt, pepper and cayenne. Add the lemon juice. Divide the soup between individual soup bowls and serve immediately.

Variation: Mouclade Proceed as for the basic soup but add 2 tsp curry powder when you add the wine. The curry adds a little warmth to the soup that is interesting and really delicious.

how to make the perfect
lobster bisque

In my opinion, this is king of the fish soups. It is creamy, rich in flavour and simply bursting with the essence of the sea. If you choose, you can make it, following the same method but with other shellfish, such as crabs, crayfish and prawns. Many chefs prefer to use live shellfish, which will undoubtedly taste better, though you will still get an excellent flavour without. Most home cooks are a little nervous of handling live shellfish so my recipe begins with a cooked lobster.

75g (2½oz/⅓ cup) unsalted butter

500g (1lb 2oz) cooked lobster, meat removed from tail and claws and shells crushed

1 celery stick, coarsely chopped

1 carrot, coarsely chopped

1 onion, coarsely chopped

2 garlic cloves, crushed

100ml (3½fl oz/scant ½ cup) brandy

3 tbsp tomato purée

75g (2½oz/½ cup) plain flour

150ml (5fl oz/⅔ cup) dry white wine

4 ripe tomatoes, coarsely chopped

1 bayleaf

1 tbsp tarragon leaves, plus extra to garnish

6 white peppercorns

1 litre (1¾ pints/4 cups) fish stock (see p.24) or white chicken stock (see p.17)

100ml (3½fl oz/scant ½ cup) double cream

sea salt and freshly ground black pepper

good pinch of cayenne pepper

1 Heat the butter in a heavy-based pan over a medium heat, then add the crushed lobster shells and fry for 5 minutes, or until lightly golden.

2 Add the celery, carrot, onion and garlic and fry for 10 minutes, or until the vegetables have coloured.

3 Pour the brandy over and set it alight to burn off the alcohol.

4 Stir in the tomato purée and mix well. Reduce the heat, then add the flour and stir with a wooden spoon. Cook, stirring continuously for 5 minutes until a roux forms around the lobster shells and the flour is cooked.

5 Pour the wine over and cook for 1 minute, then add the tomatoes, bayleaf, tarragon and peppercorns. Pour the stock over and bring to the boil, stirring occasionally.

6 Reduce the heat and simmer for 35–40 minutes, or until the soup is cooked and the flavours have been extracted from the ingredients. Skim off any impurities that float to the surface. Strain through a fine sieve.

7 Meanwhile, cut the lobster meat into bite-sized pieces. Return the strained soup to a clean pan and add the cream. Season with salt, pepper and cayenne pepper to taste.

8 Divide the lobster meat and the soup between 4 individual hot soup bowls, garnish with the remaining tarragon and serve immediately.

Variations: Lobster Bisque with Spicy Smoked Paprika Crème Fraîche Proceed as for the basic soup but replace the cayenne with smoked paprika, to taste. Instead of adding the double cream, swirl 3 tbsp crème fraîche on the surface of the soup before serving.

Creamed Lobster, Coconut, Green Tea Soup Proceed as for the basic soup but omit the white wine, replacing it with 450ml (15fl oz/2 cups) coconut milk and replacing the tarragon with fresh coriander. Also add 1 tsp green tea for the last 10 minutes of cooking. Strain the soup before serving.

6

8

This soup needs to be made over two days for the tastiest results. The bouquet garni plays an important role. You can easily make one by tying together a small bunch of thyme, a bayleaf and a few parsley stalks with a piece of kitchen string.

oxtail soup with guinness

1.5kg (3lb 3oz) oxtail, excess fat removed and cut into pieces

50g (1¾oz/⅓ cup) plain flour

50g (1¾oz/3½ tbsp) unsalted butter

2 tbsp vegetable oil

½ tbsp tomato purée

1 onion, studded with 2 cloves

2 carrots, coarsely chopped

1 celery stick, coarsely chopped

2 litres (3½ pints/8½ cups) beef stock (see p.22)

275ml (9fl oz/1¼ cups) Guinness or other dark beer

1 tbsp demerara sugar

1 bouquet garni, (see introduction)

1 tbsp redcurrant jelly

sea salt and freshly ground black pepper

The day before, dredge the oxtail pieces in a little of the flour. Heat 25g (scant 1 oz/2 tbsp) of the butter with the oil in a heavy-based pan over a medium heat. Add the oxtail pieces to the pan and fry for 8–10 minutes, stirring occasionally, or until golden all over.

Add the tomato purée, onion, carrots and celery. Cook for 5 minutes. Pour the stock, Guinness or other dark beer over, add the sugar, then bring to the boil. Reduce the heat, then add the bouquet garni and simmer, uncovered, for 3–4 hours, or until the meat is almost falling off the bones.

Remove the meat with a slotted spoon, leave to cool, then cut it into small cubes. When cool, transfer to the fridge to chill overnight.

Meanwhile, strain the stock into a bowl, discarding the vegetables and the bouquet garni. When cool, transfer to the fridge to chill overnight.

Next day, remove every vestige of fat from the top of the stock.

Heat the remaining butter in a pan over a medium heat. Reduce the heat to low, add the remaining flour and stir with a wooden spoon to make a roux. Cook, stirring continuously for 2 minutes, or until the flour is cooked.

Meanwhile, reheat the stock in a clean pan. Add the hot stock to the roux, a little at a time, stirring continuously with a wooden spoon until the mixture comes to the boil and becomes smooth.

Reduce the heat and simmer for 15 minutes, then stir in the redcurrant jelly. If the soup is too thick, add a little more stock or water.

Season to taste, add the reserved cooked oxtail, then continue to cook for a few minutes more to heat the oxtail through. Divide the soup between individual soup bowls and serve immediately.

All too often, leeks are used as a subsidiary ingredient or as an aromatic to flavour stocks and sauces. Here, combined with potato to make a wonderfully comforting soup, they take centre stage. This soup is delicious served hot or cold, depending on the time of year. The cold version is known as vichyssoise. Serve it with lots of crusty bread and just a scattering of freshly ground black pepper.

potato and leek soup

45g (1½oz/3 tbsp) unsalted butter

1 onion, coarsely chopped

300g (10oz) leeks, trimmed and sliced

600g (1lb 5oz) floury potatoes, peeled and cut into 2.5cm (1in) cubes

1 litre (1¾ pints/4 cups) vegetable stock (see p.22) or white chicken stock (see p.17)

300ml (10fl oz/1¼ cups) double cream

250ml (9fl oz/1 cup) whole milk

sea salt and freshly ground black pepper

2 tbsp snipped chives, to garnish

crusty bread, to serve

Heat 30g (1oz/2 tbsp) of the butter in a heavy-based pan over a medium heat. Add the onion and leeks and fry for about 10 minutes, or until softened. Add the potatoes and stock and bring to the boil.

Reduce the heat and simmer for about 25 minutes, or until the potatoes are just cooked. Do not overcook or the flavour will be impaired.

Transfer to a blender or use a hand-held stick blender to blitz to a smooth purée. Strain through a fine sieve.

Return the soup to a clean pan, add the cream and milk, then bring back to the boil. Whisk in the remaining butter and season to taste.

Divide the soup between individual soup bowls and serve, sprinkled with the snipped chives and some freshly ground black pepper, and accompanied by plenty of crusty bread.

Variations: Potato, Leek and Sorrel Soup Proceed as for the basic soup but add a handful of shredded sorrel leaves just before serving.

Potato Leek and Reblochon Soup Proceed as for the basic soup but add 100g (3½oz) Reblochon cheese and allow it to melt in the soup. Instead of puréeing the soup, just strain it through a sieve, then return to a clean pan over a medium heat until warmed through. Meanwhile, fry 50g (1¾oz) finely diced smoked bacon in a little oil until golden and crispy. Sprinkle the soup with the fried bacon and with chopped chives and serve immediately.

Potato, Cabbage and Cumin Soup Proceed as for the basic soup but replace the leeks with the same weight of Savoy cabbage and 1 tsp ground cumin.

THIS PAGE: Cullen Skink
(recipe page 154)

OPPOSITE: London Particular
(recipe page 155)

Scotland's equivalent of America's chowders, cullen skink's strange-sounding name comes from the fishing village of Cullen in Morayshire. It must be made with undyed smoked haddock, onions and potatoes, all cooked in a rich broth made from poaching the haddock in milk. Although not traditional, I add some soft-boiled quail eggs to my version.

cullen skink

450g (1lb) natural undyed smoked haddock (preferably Finnan haddock)

600ml (1 pint/2½ cups) whole milk, hot

2 onions, sliced

1 blade of mace (optional)

600ml (1 pint/2½ cups) fish stock (see p.24) or water

25g (scant 1oz/2 tbsp) unsalted butter

4 medium floury potatoes, peeled and cubed

6 quail eggs

sea salt and freshly ground black pepper

pinch of nutmeg

90ml (3fl oz/⅓ cup) double cream

1 tbsp finely snipped chives, to serve

Put the haddock in a pan, pour the hot milk over and add half the onions and the mace, if using. Bring to the boil, pour the stock over and bring back to the boil. Reduce the heat to a simmer and gently poach the haddock for 4–5 minutes, or until it is opaque and cooked through.

Remove the haddock with a slotted spoon. Strain the cooking liquid and set aside. Flake the haddock, removing all the skin and bones. Keep the flakes fairly chunky.

Melt the butter in a clean pan over a medium heat, add the remaining onion and cook for 8–10 minutes, or until softened. Add the potatoes and the strained cooking liquid, reduce the heat and simmer for 15 minutes, or until the potatoes are just tender.

Meanwhile, cook the quail eggs for 2½ minutes in boiling water, then remove with a slotted spoon and cool in a solution of iced water and vinegar (see Cook's secret). Once they are cool, remove the shells. Reheat the peeled eggs in a small pan of simmering water for 30 seconds.

You can now either leave the soup chunky and thick or, as I prefer, transfer it to a blender or use a hand-held stick blender and blitz until smooth. Season with salt, pepper and a pinch of nutmeg. Stir in the cream and the cooked flaked fish.

Divide the soup between 4 individual soup bowls, top each with 3 quail egg halves and sprinkle over the chives. Serve immediately.

COOK'S SECRET

Cooking the quail eggs and immersing them immediately into a solution of iced water and vinegar makes it easier to remove their shells. The acidity of the vinegar breaks down their thin membrane-like shells. It is best to leave the cooked eggs in the solution for around 30 minutes before peeling.

The origins of this winter-warming soup date back to the first half of the nineteenth century, when dense fog often filled Britain's streets, especially those of London. The result was commonly known as a London Particular, a London fog or a 'pea souper', hence the name for this thick pea and ham soup. If you prefer, you can make the soup with yellow split peas rather than green. This recipe is my more modern take on this olden-day favourite.

london particular

1 hock of smoked ham, soaked overnight in plenty of cold water, then drained

1 onion, cut in half and each half studded with 2 cloves

2 celery sticks, coarsely chopped (celery leaves reserved, to garnish)

1 bayleaf

few sprigs of thyme

25g (scant 1 oz/2 tbsp) unsalted butter

1 onion, cut into cubes

250g (9oz/1¼ cups) green split peas, picked over, soaked overnight, then drained

1 tbsp coarsely chopped mint

1 tbsp coarsely chopped flat-leaf parsley

sea salt and freshly ground black pepper

Put the ham in a large saucepan and cover with fresh cold water. Add the onion studded with cloves and the celery, bayleaf and thyme. Bring to the boil, reduce the heat and simmer, uncovered, for 2–2½ hours, or until the ham is tender.

Leave the ham to cool in the liquid, then remove. Strain the cooking liquid – you should have about 2 litres (3½ pints/8½ cups) – and set aside. Discard the vegetables. Shred the cooked ham into bite-sized pieces and set aside.

Melt the butter in a heavy-based pan over a low heat, then add the cubed onion and cook for 10 minutes, or until softened. Add the drained split peas and the cooking liquid. Bring to the boil, then reduce the heat and simmer for 45 minutes to 1 hour, or until the peas are very tender.

Transfer half the soup to a blender or use a hand-held stick blender to blitz to a smooth purée. Add a little water if the purée is too thick. Return the purée to the pan with the soup and mix well. Add the pieces of ham and the mint and parsley. Season to taste.

Divide the soup between 4 individual soup bowls, garnish with celery leaves and serve immediately.

The secret of a good Scotch broth is the really slow cooking of the meat and vegetables, making a slow cooker perhaps the best piece of kit for the job. Although not traditionally part of the recipe, I have added some haggis in the form of dumplings. Haggis is another great culinary treasure from Scotland: it's a mystery to me why it is not in the traditional recipe.

scotch broth with haggis dumplings

450g (1lb) middle neck of lamb, trimmed of all excess fat

2 litres (3½ pints/8½ cups) lamb stock (see p.22) or water

75g (2½oz/⅓ cup) pearl barley

100g (3½oz/½ cup) dried green split peas soaked overnight, then drained

1 onion, coarsely chopped

1 leek, trimmed and cut into 1cm (½in) cubes

3 carrots, cut into 1cm (½in) cubes

1 turnip, peeled and cut into 1cm (½in) cubes

1 swede, peeled and cut into 1cm (½in) cubes

2 celery sticks, shredded

1¼ small white cabbage, shredded

sea salt and freshly ground black pepper

1 tbsp coarsely chopped flat-leaf parsley

For the haggis dumplings

200g (7oz) traditional haggis, skin removed

1 egg, beaten

100g (3½oz/2 cups) fresh white breadcrumbs

100g (3½oz/1 cup) shredded vegetable suet

Put the lamb in a large pan, cover with the stock or water and bring to the boil. Skim off any impurities that float to the surface.

Add the remaining ingredients except the salt and pepper and parsley, and reduce the heat to a simmer. Cook for about 1½ hours, or until the lamb is tender. Remove the lamb and set aside to cool. Return the broth to the heat.

Meanwhile, make the haggis dumplings by mixing all the ingredients together in a bowl. Season to taste. Using wet hands, roll the mix into 1cm (½in) balls and drop them carefully into the simmering broth.

Simmer the broth for 4–5 minutes more. Shred the cooled lamb, season with salt and pepper and add to the broth. Add the parsley, then divide the soup between 4 individual soup bowls. Serve immediately.

This traditional Scottish soup dates back to the eighteenth century. It seems that all the early recipes contained prunes, though some included raisins instead. There should be just a hint of a sweet element to the soup. In Scotland, cock-a-leekie is often garnished with pieces of fried bread.

cock-a-leekie

250g (9oz/2 cups) Agen prunes, pitted

150ml (5fl oz/²⁄₃ cup) freshly brewed tea

1.5kg (3lb 3oz) chicken, jointed and skin removed

550g (1¼lb) shin of beef or stewing beef, cut into 2cm (¾in) cubes

1kg (2¼lb) young leeks, trimmed and thinly sliced, using as much of the green leaves as possible

150g (5½oz/¾ cup) cooked long-grain rice

1 tbsp coarsely chopped flat-leaf parsley

sea salt and freshly ground black pepper

Put the prunes in a bowl, cover with the hot tea and soak for 1 hour. Drain and set aside.

Put the chicken and beef in a large pan, cover with water and bring to the boil. Reduce the heat, then add the leeks. Simmer for 45 minutes, or until the chicken and beef are cooked through. Skim off any impurities that float to the surface.

Remove the chicken and beef with a slotted spoon and leave to cool. Add the soaked prunes to the soup, together with the cooked rice. Simmer for 5 minutes more.

Meanwhile, remove the chicken from the bones and shred. Return the shredded chicken and the beef to the soup and stir in the parsley. Season to taste. Divide the soup between 4 individual soup bowls and serve immediately.

In Morocco this soup is traditionally served as part of the Ramadan festivities, to break the fast. Packed with warm Moroccan flavours, it makes a delicious first course or a hearty meal on its own. For a contemporary twist, serve with some small sweet date pasties, known as *borek*; they make a lovely accompaniment. Brik pastry is a very thin pastry from the Mahgreb, especially Tunisia.

al harira with date pasties

100g (3½oz/½ cup) dried chickpeas, soaked overnight, then drained

100g (3½oz/½ cup) Puy lentils

400g (14oz) lamb rump, all fat removed and cut into 1cm (½in) cubes

1 onion, finely chopped

1 tsp ground turmeric

1 tsp ground cumin

½ tsp ground cinnamon

2.5cm (1in) piece of root ginger, finely chopped

1 tsp paprika

good pinch of saffron strands

1.5 litres (2¾ pints/1.3 quarts) lamb stock (see p.22) or white chicken stock (see p.17)

50g (1¾oz/3½ tbsp) unsalted butter

2 tbsp coarsely chopped fresh coriander

1 x 400g (14oz) can chopped tomatoes in juice

100g (3½oz) vermicelli

sea salt and freshly ground black pepper

2 eggs

30g (1oz/¼ cup) plain flour

juice of ½ lemon

lemon halves, to serve

For the date pasties

100g (3½oz/½ cup) dates, pitted and coarsely chopped

50g (1¾oz/½ cup) walnuts, coarsely chopped

good pinch of ground cumin

2 sheets of brik or spring roll pastry

1 egg, lightly beaten, for the egg wash

Put the chickpeas and lentils in a large pan and add the lamb, onion and spices. Pour the lamb or chicken stock over and bring to the boil. Skim off any impurities that float to the surface, reduce the heat and simmer, uncovered, for 1½–2 hours, or until the lamb and chickpeas are tender. Add a little more water if necessary.

Meanwhile, make the date pasties. Preheat the oven to 180°C (350°F/ Gas 4). Mix the dates, walnuts and cumin in a bowl. Lay the sheets of pastry on the work surface, cut each into 4 squares and brush liberally with the egg wash.

Place a spoonful of the date mixture on a pastry square, in the half that is furthest from you. Fold the end of the pastry square that is nearest to you over the mixture, fold in the sides, then roll the pastry up to form a spring-roll shape. Repeat with the remaining squares of pastry and date mixture to make 8 rolls in total.

Place the rolls on a baking sheet, brush with egg wash again, then place in the preheated oven. Bake for 7–8 minutes, or until golden. Remove from the oven and leave to cool a little.

Fifteen minutes before the time is up for simmering the stock, add the butter, coriander, tomatoes and vermicelli. Season to taste and return to a simmer.

Meanwhile, in a bowl, mix the eggs with the flour and 100ml (3½fl oz/ scant ½ cup) water. Stir this into the soup and cook for 1 minute. The soup will thicken slightly. Add the lemon juice.

Divide the soup between 4 individual soup bowls and serve immediately with the date pasties and with a lemon half for each person to squeeze over their soup, to taste.

This great French classic is a fresh vegetable soup from Provence. Never has a blending of simple vegetables and fresh herbs tasted so good. Finishing the soup with the fresh basil pesto adds a flavour explosion that will live in your memory. Soupe au Pistou is equally delicious served cold on a hot day.

soupe au pistou

1 large potato

2 carrots

2 small leeks, white part only

1 onion

2 celery sticks

1 courgette

1 tbsp extra virgin olive oil

1.5 litres (2¾ pints/1.3 quarts) hot white chicken stock (see p.17)

sea salt and freshly ground black pepper

For the pesto

20 large basil leaves

2 tbsp pine nuts, toasted

1 garlic clove, crushed

50g (1¾oz/½ cup) Parmesan cheese, finely grated

60ml (2fl oz/¼ cup) extra virgin olive oil

Prepare the vegetables. Peel the potato and carrots. Cut the leeks, onion, celery, courgette, potato and carrots into 1cm (½in) cubes.

In a heavy-based pan, heat the oil with 2 tbsp water over a medium heat. Add the cubed vegetables and cook gently over a medium-low heat for 5 minutes, or until all the water has evaporated. Do not allow the vegetables to brown.

Pour the hot stock over, bring to the boil, reduce the heat and simmer gently for 25–30 minutes, or until the vegetables are just tender.

Meanwhile, make the pesto. Place all the ingredients in a small blender and blitz to a smooth paste.

Add the pesto to the soup and stir thoroughly. Do not allow the soup to come to the boil again. Season to taste.

Divide the soup between 4 individual soup bowls and serve immediately.

Variation: Asian Pesto Soup Proceed as for the basic soup but add a 2.5cm (1in) piece of root ginger with the cubed vegetables. Finish the soup with an Asian-inspired pesto, made by blitzing the following together in a blender: 100ml (3½fl oz/scant ½ cup) peanut oil; 20g (¾oz) mint; 20g (¾oz) coriander leaves; 45g (1½oz) Thai basil, 50g (1¾oz/⅓ cup) peanuts, lightly roasted; 1 garlic clove, crushed; 1 tsp fish sauce (nam pla); 1 tsp sugar and the juice of ½ lime.

From Greece, this traditional, easy-to-make, tasty chicken soup can be served cold or hot. Avgolemeno is also the name for a warm Greek sauce made with egg yolks and lemon that is often served with vegetables, lamb meatballs or stuffed vine leaves. Although it isn't traditional to do so, I like to add some orzo pasta – a rice-shaped pasta – together with a little shredded cooked chicken. Grated lemon zest added at the end provides a burst of freshness.

avgolemeno

1 litre (1¾ pints/4 cups) white chicken stock (see p.17)

100g (3½oz) orzo pasta

3 small eggs

3 tbsp double cream

juice of 1 small lemon

1 tsp grated lemon zest

2 small cooked chicken breasts, skin removed and flesh finely shredded

sea salt and freshly ground black pepper

Put the stock in a pan over a medium heat, bring to the boil and add the pasta. Reduce the heat and simmer for 15–18 minutes, or until the pasta is al dente. Remove the pasta with a slotted spoon, reserving the cooking liquid.

Meanwhile, lightly beat the eggs in a bowl with the cream and lemon juice. Gradually pour 5–6 tbsp of the pasta cooking liquid into the egg mixture, beating continuously.

Return the egg mixture to the remaining cooking liquid and immediately remove from the heat, stirring continuously. Do not allow the soup to come to the boil or it will curdle.

Return the pasta to the soup and add the lemon zest and shredded chicken. Season to taste. Divide the soup between 4 individual soup bowls and serve immediately.

Like all good thick soups, this one tastes better after a few days. There are many recipes for minestrone both in and outside of Italy, but I was always taught that, whatever else minestrone contains, you have to include some broken pieces of spaghetti that are cooked in the soup.

classic minestrone

3 tbsp extra virgin olive oil

150g (5½oz) pancetta, cut into 1cm (½in) cubes

2 medium carrots, cut into 1cm (½in) cubes

1 onion, cut into 1cm (½in) cubes

2 celery sticks, trimmed, peeled and cut into 1cm (½in) cubes

3 garlic cloves, crushed, plus a little extra to rub on the bread

750g (1¾oz) Savoy cabbage, stalks removed and leaves coarsely chopped

125g (4½oz) French beans, trimmed and cut into 1cm (½in) lengths

1 x 400g (14oz) can chopped tomatoes in juice

1 tsp thyme leaves

6 sage leaves, coarsely chopped

900ml (1½ pints/4 cups) white chicken stock (see p.17) or vegetable stock (see p.22)

400g (14oz/2¼ cups) freshly cooked or canned cannellini beans, drained and rinsed

75g (2½oz) spaghetti, broken into 1cm (½in) lengths

½ baguette or crusty loaf, cut into cubes, for the croûtons

freshly grated Parmesan cheese, to garnish

Heat 2 tbsp of the oil in a large heavy-based pan over a medium heat, then add the pancetta and fry for 4–5 minutes, or until golden. Add the carrots, onion, celery and garlic, reduce the heat and cook, stirring frequently, for 8–10 minutes, or until the vegetables are lightly caramelised.

Add the cabbage, beans, tomatoes, thyme, sage and stock. Bring to the boil. Reduce the heat and simmer for 30 minutes, or until the vegetables are tender. Add a little more stock if needed, but not too much as the soup should be thick.

Add the beans and spaghetti and cook for 15 minutes more, or until the pasta is al dente.

Meanwhile, make the croûtons. Heat the grill and rub the bread cubes with the remaining garlic. Put the cubes on the grill pan. Drizzle with the remaining oil and put under the grill until golden.

Divide the soup between 4 individual soup bowls and serve immediately with the croûtons and a scattering of Parmesan cheese.

Variation: Green Minestrone This is a great summer variation. Proceed as for the basic soup but omit the pancetta and replace the carrots, celery and cabbage with courgettes, peas, broad beans and spinach. Before serving, stir in 2 tbsp coarsely chopped fresh basil, together with the garlic bread cubes and the Parmesan cheese.

This recipe really is truly wonderful. It is mildly spicy and creamy, and extremely delicate. I love the use of the rice krispies to make the sweet croûtons that are served with the soup. Atul is a friend, TV personality, restaurateur and inspirational chef who is doing great work in bringing modern Indian cuisine to the British public.

ATUL KOCHHAR'S
mulligatawny with rice crisps

350g (12oz/1¾ cups) masoor dal (split red lentils)

100ml (3½fl oz/scant ½ cup) coconut oil

20g (¾oz) curry leaves

2 dried red chillies

200g (7oz/1¾ cups) onion, medium sliced

50g (1¾oz/⅓ cup) carrot, cut into cubes

45g (1½oz/½ cup) celery, trimmed and cut into cubes

3 garlic cloves, crushed

30g (1oz) fresh root ginger, finely chopped

100g (3½oz) Granny Smith apple, peeled, cored and cut into cubes

1 tbsp crushed black pepper

sea salt, to taste

Madras curry powder, to taste

2 litres (3½ pints/8½ cups) lamb stock (see p.22) or white chicken stock (see p.17)

750–1000ml (1¼–1¾ pints/3–4 cups) coconut milk

juice of 1 lemon

For the rice crisps

100g (3½oz) white marshmallows

60g (2oz/¼ cup) unsalted butter

150g (10½oz/1⅔ cups) desiccated coconut

50g (1¾oz) fried curry leaves

150g (10½oz/5⅓ cups) rice krispies

1 tbsp chilli powder

25g (scant 1oz) chaat masala

sea salt, to taste

The day before, prepare the rice crisps. Melt the marshmallows and butter together in a pan over a low heat. Add the remaining ingredients, stirring frequently to ensure the mixture doesn't catch on the bottom of the pan.

When all the ingredients have been incorporated, put the mixture in a tray and leave to set, about 1 hour. Keep in a dry place until ready to serve.

The next day, wash the masoor dal and set aside.

Heat the coconut oil in a large pan over a medium heat, then add the curry leaves and dried chillies. Cook for 1 minute, or until the curry leaves have become crispy, then add the onion, carrot, celery, garlic, ginger and apple. Reduce the heat to low and cook for 2–3 minutes more.

Add the masoor dal and season with black pepper, salt and curry powder. Add the lamb or chicken stock, reduce the heat and simmer for 30 minutes, or until the lentils are soft. Add the coconut milk and simmer for 10 minutes more.

Transfer to a blender or use a hand-held stick blender and blitz to a purée. Strain through a fine sieve and add lemon juice to taste. Return to the pan and bring to the boil.

Remove the rice crisps from the tray and cut into small 1cm (½in) cubes.

Divide the soup between 4 individual soup bowls and serve immediately, garnished with the rice crisps.

wild and exotic

My late father was a great lover of mussels. As a child, I remember him anticipating the start of the mussel season with great excitement. Although he loved them plainly steamed in their own juices, I know he would have approved of this recipe, with its aromas of the Orient.

mussel soup with thai gremolata

1kg (2¼lb) fresh mussels in their shells

2.5cm (1in) piece of root ginger, thinly sliced

2 garlic cloves, crushed

2 bananas shallots, thinly sliced

750ml (1¼ pints/3 cups) fish stock (see p.24)

200ml (7fl oz/¾ cup) coconut milk

1 tbsp fish sauce (nam pla)

pinch of ground turmeric

1 tbsp palm sugar or brown sugar

1 tbsp tamarind paste

For the thai gremolata

1 garlic clove, crushed

2 tbsp coarsely chopped coriander

2 tbsp coarsely chopped Thai basil

grated zest of ½ lime

grated zest of ½ lemon

1 small bird's eye chilli, finely chopped

Wash the mussels carefully, removing any sand and beards. Discard any mussels that are open as they are dead. Set aside.

Put the ginger, garlic and shallots in a pan, pour the stock over and bring to the boil. Reduce the heat, then add the coconut milk, fish sauce, turmeric, sugar and tamarind paste. Simmer gently for 15 minutes, or until the soup is infused with the flavours and smells fragrant.

Meanwhile, make the gremolata by mixing all the ingredients together in a small bowl. Set aside.

Add the mussels to the pan with the soup, cover with a lid and simmer for 3–4 minutes, or until the mussels have opened. Discard any mussels that have not opened as these are also dead.

Divide the mussels between 4 deep individual soup bowls. Pour the hot soup over, scatter with the Thai gremolata and serve immediately.

tom khai gai

Another spicy flavoured *tom*, or broth, from Thailand, mellowed with coconut milk. I prefer to make this soup the day before it is served. It is a wonderful soup packed with flavour. Galangal is a noble, camphor-flavoured ginger, quite different from normal root ginger and readily available in good supermarkets and Asian stores. Root ginger can be used as a substitute if necessary.

salmon, sweetcorn and edamame soup

In Asia, many soups contain some sort of noodle, making them a healthy main meal. For this Japanese-themed soup, it is vital to establish a well-flavoured broth for the base. As salmon has a very soft, delicate flesh, only add it to the soup at the very last minute so it stays juicy and moist. Japanese green-tea noodles are available from good Japanese or Asian stores but egg noodles can be substituted.

green curry soup with smoked tofu

Tofu is widely used in vegan and vegetarian diets. It is made by coagulating soy juice, then pressing the resulting curds into soft white blocks, similar to making cheese. The most common varieties are silken tofu and firm tofu, as well as the less well-known smoked tofu, used in this recipe. Smoked tofu is an interesting variation that adds the smokiness to this spicy curry soup. Use firm tofu if smoked tofu is unavailable.

chinese roast pork soup with meatballs

Cantonese-style roast pork, better known as *char siu*, is made by cooking marinated strips of pork skewered on long forks over a hot fire, which gives it its barbecue flavour. I take the easy route by buying it at a Chinese deli or restaurant. This makes the soup less time-consuming. I don't think you ever get the authentic flavour when you make your own.

OPPOSITE Top left: Tom Khai Gai (recipe page 176); top right: Salmon, Sweetcorn and Edamame Soup (recipe page 176); bottom left: Green Curry Soup with Smoked Tofu (recipe page 177); bottom right: Chinese Roast Pork Soup with Meatballs (recipe page 177)

tom khai gai

1 tbsp peanut or sunflower oil

400ml (14fl oz/1¾ cups) coconut milk

½ tbsp red Thai curry paste

600ml (1 pint/2½ cups) Asian chicken stock (see p.17) or white chicken stock (see p.17)

2.5cm (1in) piece galangal, peeled and thinly sliced

2 small red bird's eye chillies, thinly sliced

3 stalks of lemongrass, tough outer layers removed and the rest thinly sliced

6 kaffir lime leaves, shredded

4 sprigs of coriander, roots and stems

150g (5½oz/2⅓ cups) shiitake mushrooms, thinly sliced

400g (14oz) boneless chicken breast, skin removed and thinly sliced

1 tbsp palm sugar or brown sugar

1 tbsp fish sauce (nam pla)

juice of 1 lime

2 small shallots, thinly sliced

4 spring onions, shredded

2 tbsp coarsely chopped coriander leaves

Heat the oil in a large pan over a medium heat, then add the coconut milk and curry paste and fry for 5 minutes.

Add the stock, galangal, chillies, 2 of the lemongrass stalks, half the kaffir lime leaves and the coriander roots and stems. Bring to the boil, then reduce the heat and simmer for 15 minutes, or until the soup becomes wonderfully fragrant.

Strain the soup through a fine sieve into a clean pan. Add the mushrooms, sliced chicken, sugar, fish sauce and lime juice. Cook gently over a medium heat for 8 minutes, or until the chicken is cooked through.

To serve, stir in the remaining lemongrass and kaffir lime leaves, the shallots, spring onions and chopped coriander. Divide the soup between 4 individual soup bowls and serve immediately.

salmon, sweetcorn and edamame soup

125g (4½oz) dried green-tea noodles

600ml (1 pint/2½ cups) Asian fish stock (see p.24) or fish stock (see p.24)

500g (1lb 2oz) salmon bones (from your fishmonger), cut into large pieces

2.5cm (1in) piece of root ginger, thinly sliced

1 carrot, thinly sliced

125g (4½oz/½ cup) canned or frozen sweetcorn (if using canned sweetcorn, rinse and drain)

1 small red chilli, thinly sliced

125g (4½oz) fresh or frozen edamame beans (shelled weight)

1 tbsp mirin or sugar

2 tsp white miso paste

1 tbsp tamari (Japanese soy sauce) or soy sauce

1 tbsp fish sauce (nam pla)

400g (14oz) salmon fillet, skin removed and cut into 2.5cm (1in) cubes

2 spring onions, shredded

½ small iceberg lettuce, leaves separated and shredded

Cook the noodles in a large pan of boiling salted water for 5–7 minutes, or until just tender. Drain in a colander and rinse under cold water to refresh and set aside.

Put the stock and 300ml (10fl oz/1¼ cups) water in a large pan, add the salmon bones, bring to the boil then reduce the heat. Simmer on the lowest setting for 10 minutes. Carefully strain the broth into a clean pan through a fine sieve. Discard the bones.

Return the broth to the heat and add the ginger, carrot, sweetcorn, chilli and edamame beans, together with the mirin or sugar, the miso paste, the tamari or soy sauce and the fish sauce. Cook for 5 minutes over a medium heat to infuse the broth with the flavours.

Reduce the heat, then add the salmon fillet and the spring onions. Simmer for 2 minutes.

Divide the noodles between 4 individual soup bowls and top with the shredded lettuce. Carefully pour the hot salmon broth over and serve immediately.

green curry soup with smoked tofu and crispy shallots

3 tbsp peanut or sunflower oil

8 banana shallots, thinly sliced

2 garlic cloves, crushed

2 stalks of lemongrass, tough outer layers removed and the rest finely chopped

1 tbsp green Thai curry paste

400ml (14fl oz/1¾ cups) coconut milk

200ml (7fl oz/¾ cup) vegetable stock (see p.22)

200g (7oz/3 cups) shiitake mushrooms, sliced, stalks discarded

350g (12oz) firm smoked tofu, cut into batons or cubes

1 tbsp tamari (Japanese soy sauce)

600ml (1 pint/2½ cups) sunflower oil, for deep-frying

sea salt

handful of baby spinach, leaves only

2 sheets of nori seaweed, shredded

2 tbsp cooked basmati rice

25g (scant 1oz) coriander leaves

2 tbsp coarsely chopped roasted peanuts

Heat a large pan with 1 tbsp of the oil over a low heat. Add a quarter of the shallots, the garlic and the lemongrass and cook for 2 minutes, or until fragrant. Add the curry paste and cook for 2–3 minutes, stirring continuously. Pour the coconut milk and the stock over and bring to the boil. Reduce the heat, then add the mushrooms and simmer for 10 minutes.

Meanwhile, heat the remaining oil in a wok or large frying pan over a medium heat, then add the tofu and stir-fry for 1 minute. Add the tamari and stir to coat the tofu. Set aside.

Heat a deep pan with the sunflower oil to 160°C (325°F). Add the remaining shallots and fry quickly until golden and crispy. Remove with a slotted spoon onto kitchen paper to drain. Sprinkle with a little salt.

Add the spinach and nori seaweed to the soup and simmer until wilted.

Divide the soup between 4 individual soup bowls. Top each with the fried tofu, a scattering of crispy-fried shallots, the cooked rice, coriander and chopped roasted peanuts. Serve immediately.

chinese roast pork soup with meatballs

1 litre (1¾ pints/4 cups) Asian chicken stock (see p.17)

3 tbsp Chinese rice wine or dry sherry

1 tbsp soy sauce

1 tsp caster sugar

2.5cm (1in) piece of root ginger, thinly sliced

225g (8oz) canned bamboo shoots, rinsed and drained

1 red chilli, thinly sliced

2 baby bok choi, leaves separated

1 tbsp cornflour

300g (10oz) Chinese barbecued roast pork (char siu), shredded

2 spring onions, shredded

sesame oil, for drizzling

For the meatballs

225g (8oz/2 cups) minced pork

2.5cm (1in) piece of root ginger, finely chopped

1 small red chilli, deseeded and finely chopped

2 spring onions, shredded

2 tbsp coarsely chopped coriander

2 tbsp hoisin sauce

1 tbsp soy sauce

1 tsp ground coriander

Firstly prepare the meatballs. Put all the ingredients in a bowl, mix well to combine, then refrigerate, covered with clingfilm, while you prepare the soup.

For the soup, put the stock in a large pan and add the rice wine or sherry, soy sauce, sugar and ginger. Bring to the boil, then reduce the heat and simmer for 5 minutes. Add the bamboo shoots, chilli and bok choi and simmer for 5 minutes more.

Mix the cornflour with 2 tbsp cold water in a bowl, then stir into the hot soup to thicken it lightly.

Remove the meatball mix from the fridge and, using wet hands, drop 1cm (½in) diameter balls into the soup. Simmer for 10 minutes, or until cooked. Add the shredded pork, then divide the soup between 4 individual soup bowls. Scatter with the shredded spring onions and add a drizzle of sesame oil. Serve immediately.

Some of the ingredients for Crab Laksa (recipe pages 180–183)

how to make the perfect
crab laksa

Laksa is a popular spicy soup of Malaysian and Chinese origin. I first tasted it while working in Singapore in the late 1980s. The flavour remains in my memory to this day; it was a real taste experience. Laksa is thought to have been named after the Chinese word for 'spicy sand' – no doubt a reference to the sandy-textured laksa spice paste that is the base of this coconut-flavoured soup.

1 tbsp peanut or vegetable oil

2 garlic cloves, crushed

2 red chillies, cut in half, deseeded and finely chopped

150ml (5fl oz/⅔ cup) Asian fish stock (see p.24)

600ml (1 pint/2½ cups) coconut milk

4 spring onions, shredded

juice of ½ lime

1 tbsp fish sauce (nam pla)

1 tbsp palm sugar or brown sugar

2 stalks of lemongrass, tough outer layers removed and the rest finely chopped

3 kaffir lime leaves, finely shredded

200g (7oz) rice stick noodles

100g (3½oz/1 cup) beansprouts

350g (12oz/1½ cups) fresh white crabmeat

25g (scant 1oz/1 cup) mint or coriander leaves, to garnish

halves of lime, to serve

For the laksa paste

1 tsp red chilli flakes

25g (scant 1oz) dried shrimp paste

50g (1¾oz/⅓ cup) cashew nuts

1 garlic clove

2cm (¾in) piece of root ginger, grated

1 tsp ground turmeric

1 Firstly prepare the laksa paste. Put the chilli flakes and shrimp paste in a bowl, add 3 tbsp hot water, cover with clingfilm and leave to soften for 30 minutes.

2 Drain, then put into a mortar and pestle or a small blender together with the cashew nuts, garlic, ginger and turmeric. Grind together to form a coarse, sandy-textured paste, then set aside. You should have about 150g (5½oz) laksa paste.

3 For the soup, heat the oil in a small pan over a medium heat, then add the garlic and chillies and cook for 1 minute to release their fragrance. Add the stock, bring to the boil, then reduce the heat and simmer for 30 minutes, or until the stock is infused with the flavours.

4 Meanwhile, heat a small dry wok or frying pan until very hot, then add the prepared laksa paste. Stir-fry continuously for 1 minute, then add the coconut milk and spring onions.

5 Stir in the lime juice, fish sauce, sugar, lemongrass and kaffir lime leaves. Add this mixture to the simmering stock and simmer for 10 minutes more.

6 Meanwhile, add the noodles to a pan of boiling water, then remove from the heat. Leave the noodles in the water for 5 minutes, then drain.

7 Divide the beansprouts, noodles and crabmeat between 4 deep soup bowls. Ladle the hot soup over, top with the mint or coriander and serve very hot accompanied by lime halves.

THIS PAGE: Ethiopian Yam, Peanut
and Ginger Soup (recipe page 187)

OPPOSITE: Taiwanese Beef Soup
with Pickled Mustard Greens
(recipe page 186)

The star anise and dried tangerine peel add a really exotic note to this Taiwanese soup. I often like to replace the beef with some cubed chicken thigh; though this is not traditionally correct, the resulting soup is still excellent and very tasty. Pickled mustard greens are available from Asian grocers and specialist shops, usually in canned or vacuum-packed form.

taiwanese beef soup with pickled mustard greens

800g (1¾lb) stewing beef (such as chuck or skirt), fat and sinew removed and cut into 2.5cm (1in) cubes

1 litre (1¾ pints/4 cups) beef stock (see p.22) or brown chicken stock (see p.19)

100ml (3½fl oz/scant ½ cup) dark soy sauce

3 tbsp Chinese rice wine or dry sherry

4 star anise

3 garlic cloves, crushed

2.5cm (1in) piece of root ginger, thinly sliced

4 pieces of dried tangerine peel, finely shredded or ½ tsp grated orange zest

½ tsp red chilli flakes

200g (7oz) Chinese egg noodles

100ml (3½fl oz/scant ½ cup) oyster sauce

sea salt

2 tbsp brown sugar, or to taste

4 small bok choy, leaves separated

200g (7oz) canned pickled Chinese greens, drained and shredded

8 red cherry tomatoes, cut in half

25g (scant 1oz) micro coriander cress, to garnish

Put the beef in a large pan, cover with cold water and bring to the boil. Reduce the heat and simmer for 5 minutes. Skim off any impurities that float to the surface.

Remove the beef and discard the water. Transfer the beef to a clean pan, add the stock, half the soy sauce, the rice wine or sherry, the star anise, garlic, ginger, tangerine peel and half the chilli flakes. Bring to the boil. Reduce the heat and simmer for 1–1½ hours, or until the beef is tender.

Meanwhile, cook the noodles in a pan of boiling salted water for 5–6 minutes, or until just tender. Drain in a colander and set aside.

Remove the beef from the soup with a slotted spoon and set aside. Strain the soup through a fine sieve into a clean pan. Add the remaining soy sauce, the oyster sauce and a little salt and sugar to taste.

Divide the drained noodles between 4 individual soup bowls.

Return the cooked beef to the soup, add the bok choy and the remaining chilli, together with the pickled mustard greens and the tomatoes. Bring back to the boil.

Pour the soup over the noodles in the bowls and garnish with micro coriander cress. Serve immediately.

Yams are often confused with sweet potatoes and vice versa. They are starchier and drier than sweet potatoes. Yams are found throughout tropical America, especially in Peru and Ecuador as well as in parts of Asia. Nowadays yams can be easily sourced nearer to home from ethnic Caribbean markets. Sweet potato also works well in this African-inspired peanut soup.

ethiopian yam, peanut and ginger soup

2 tbsp peanut oil

1 onion, coarsely chopped

2cm (¾in) piece of root ginger, grated

1 garlic clove, crushed

½ tsp red chilli powder

½ tsp ground cumin

½ tsp ground coriander

400g (14oz) yellow or white yam, peeled and coarsely chopped

1 litre (1¾ pints/4 cups) white chicken stock (see p.17)

75g (2½oz/¼ cup) smooth peanut butter

400ml (14fl oz/1¾ cups) coconut milk

juice of 1 lime

sea salt and freshly ground black pepper

50g (1¾oz/⅓ cup) roasted peanuts, coarsely chopped, to garnish

Heat the oil in a large pan over the lowest heat, then add the onion, ginger and garlic together with the chilli powder, cumin and coriander. Cook for 10 minutes, or until the onion is softened.

Add the yam and stock and bring to the boil. Reduce the heat and simmer for 20–25 minutes, or until the yam is tender.

Transfer to a blender or use a hand-held stick blender to blitz to a smooth purée. Strain through a fine sieve into a clean pan. Set aside.

Heat together the peanut butter and 100ml (3½fl oz/scant ½ cup) water in a small pan and whisk until smooth and creamy.

Add the coconut milk to the sieved soup, return to the heat and bring back to the boil. Remove from the heat and whisk in the lime juice. Season to taste.

Divide the soup between 4 individual soup bowls. Drizzle a spoonful of the whisked peanut butter over each, sprinkle with the roasted peanuts and serve immediately.

This recipe comes from friend and TV celebrity chef, Tom Kerridge. It is an explosion of fresh clean flavours. Tom recently cooked this soup as part of a menu for 1,000 chefs and other industry notables, which is no mean feat. The soup was a big hit, so I am really pleased to be able to include it in my book.

TOM KERRIDGE'S
smoked apple soup with eel, bacon and mint oil

5 Bramley apples

600ml (1 pint/2½ cups) water

juice of ½ lemon

50g (1¾oz/¼ cup) caster sugar

20g (¾oz/1½ tbsp) smoked butter, chilled and cut into small cubes

For the dill-pickled cucumber

100g (3½oz/½ cup) caster sugar

200ml (7fl oz/¾ cup) white wine vinegar

½ cinnamon stick

4 star anise

2 cloves

¼ tsp fennel seeds

½ tsp coriander seeds

½ cucumber, halved lengthways, deseeded and cut into 1cm (½in) cubes

1 tbsp fresh dill

For the mint oil

75ml (2½fl oz/⅓ cup) vegetable oil

20g (¾oz/1 cup) whole mint leaves

To serve

200g (7oz) boiled cooked belly pork, rind removed and cut into 1cm (½in) cubes

200g (7oz) good-quality smoked eel fillet, skin removed and cut into 1cm (½in) cubes

75g (2½oz/2½ cups) multi-grain bread croûtons, toasted (see p.11)

borage flowers and cress (optional)

The day before, prepare the dill-pickled cucumber. Put all the ingredients except the cucumber and dill in a small pan, bring slowly to the boil, then reduce the heat and infuse for 20 minutes.

Strain through a sieve, then transfer to a small blender, add the dill and blitz until well blended. Add the cucumber and refrigerate overnight.

For the mint oil, heat the oil in a small pan to 150°C (300°F), add the mint leaves, then strain into a bowl through a sieve lined with muslin. Refrigerate until needed.

To make the soup, peel, core and thickly slice 4 of the apples. Bring the water, lemon juice and sugar to the boil, add the apples and cook for 10 minutes, or until soft.

Transfer to a blender or use a hand-held stick blender to blitz to a smooth purée. Strain through a fine sieve.

Preheat the oven to its lowest setting.

Return the strained soup to a clean pan over a medium heat and whisk in the smoked butter.

Meanwhile, put the belly pork and eel together in a small dish in the preheated oven for 2–3 minutes until warm.

Peel, core and cut the remaining apple into small cubes the same size as the eel and bacon cubes.

Divide the apple and the warmed pork and eel between the individual soup bowls, add some of the dill-pickled cucumber to each bowl, then pour the warm soup over.

Drizzle with the mint oil and scatter with the croûtons. Garnish with the borage flowers and cress, if using. Serve immediately.

Hedgerows and woodlands can offer an exciting abundance of culinary ingredients. When picking and handling nettles, always wear protective gloves to avoid being stung. Once the nettles are cooked, they lose their stinging properties. Nettles are best picked between March and April; after that, they tend to become more fibrous. This recipe is a real marriage of rich and poor – the poor man's nettle soup topped with the rich man's delicate foie gras set on shards of crispy Melba toast. The foie gras may cost a little but the soup is virtually free. The only cost is a little discomfort!

nettle soup with foie gras toasts

50g (1¾oz/3½ tbsp) unsalted butter

1 onion, coarsely chopped

1 garlic clove, crushed

3 medium leeks, trimmed and shredded

1 litre (1¾ pints/4 cups) vegetable stock (see p.22)

100g (3½oz/1 cup) oatmeal

2 large potatoes, peeled and cut into chunks

400g (14oz) young stinging nettles (picked with care!)

100ml (3½fl oz/scant ½ cup) double cream

sea salt and freshly ground black pepper

For the foie gras toasts

4 medium slices of white bread

4 thin slices of foie gras terrine

Heat 25g (scant 1oz/2 tbsp) of the butter in a large pan over a medium-low heat, then add the onion, garlic and leeks and cook for 10 minutes, or until the vegetables are softened.

Pour the stock over, bring to the boil, then add the oatmeal and potatoes. Reduce the heat and simmer for 25 minutes, or until the potatoes are tender.

Meanwhile, start the foie gras toasts. Preheat the grill. Cut the crusts from the bread to form squares, then grill lightly until golden on both sides. Slice each square in half horizontally, then diagonally into triangles. Return to the grill until golden and curled up at the edges. Set these Melba toasts aside.

With gloved hands, carefully throw the nettles into the pan containing the stock, oatmeal and potatoes. Simmer for 5 minutes only, then transfer to a blender or use a hand-held stick blender to blitz to a smooth purée.

Strain the soup through a fine sieve into a clean pan. Bring back to the boil, add the cream and whisk in the remaining butter. Season to taste.

Carefully spread a little foie gras onto each Melba toast. Divide the soup between 4 individual soup bowls and add 2 foie gras toasts to each. Sprinkle over a little salt and black pepper and serve immediately.

COOK'S SECRET

This nettle soup will freeze well, so you may wish to prepare a batch during early spring when the nettles are young and fresh. Add the cream to the soup when you serve it.

This soup may sound a little fancy, even time-consuming, but the end results are well worth the effort. You can prepare the gnocchi and the soup the day before, then cook the gnocchi just before serving and add to the soup at the last minute. If it is difficult to obtain game, try making it with rabbit; both are delicious.

autumn game bisque with chestnut gnocchi and girolle mushrooms

1 small oven-ready pheasant

1 oven-ready partridge

2 tbsp sunflower oil

25g (scant 1oz/2 tbsp) unsalted butter

1 onion, coarsely chopped

1 carrot, coarsely chopped

1 celery stick, coarsely chopped

2 sprigs of thyme

25g (scant 1oz/¼ cup) plain flour

100ml (3½fl oz/scant ½ cup) dry white wine

1.5 litres (2¾ pints/1.3 quarts) brown chicken stock (see p.19)

200g (7oz) frozen or vacuum-packed chestnuts

150g (5½oz) small girolle mushrooms, cleaned

2 tbsp redcurrant jelly

100ml (3½fl oz/scant ½ cup) double cream

1 tbsp truffle oil (optional)

For the gnocchi

175g (6oz/¾ cup) hot, dry mashed potato

15g (½oz/¼ cup) ground walnuts

20g (¾oz) unsweetened canned chestnut purée

1 tbsp unsalted butter

1 large egg yolk

75g (2½oz/½ cup) plain flour, plus extra for dusting

sea salt and pepper

Firstly start the gnocchi. Ensure the mashed potato is hot. If it isn't, microwave it for 30 seconds. Put the potato in a large bowl, add the walnuts, chestnut purée, butter, egg yolk, half the flour and salt and pepper. Mix to a smooth, stiff-textured dough.

Turn the dough out onto a floured work surface and knead in the remaining flour for about 2 minutes to form a smooth dough. Return the dough to the bowl, cover with clingfilm and refrigerate while you make the bisque.

For the bisque, remove the legs and breasts from the pheasant and partridge. Chop the legs into small pieces and remove the skin. Skin the breasts and cut into 1cm (½in) cubes. Set the breast meat aside.

Put the legs and carcasses in a pan with the oil over a medium heat. Fry until golden. Add the butter, onion, carrot, celery and thyme and fry for 10 minutes more until the vegetables are caramelised and golden.

Reduce the heat, then add the flour and stir with a wooden spoon to make a roux around the bones and vegetables. Cook, stirring continuously for about 3 minutes, or until the flour is cooked.

Pour the wine over, bring to the boil and boil for 2 minutes, then pour the stock over and bring back to the boil. Reduce the heat, then add the chestnuts and half the mushrooms. Simmer for 30 minutes.

Meanwhile, return to the gnocchi. Remove the dough from the fridge and roll it out into 1cm (½in) cylinders. Use a sharp knife to cut the cylinders into 1cm (½in) lengths. You can either leave them as they are or, more traditionally, roll each piece over the back of the tines of a fork to decorate them. Place on a tray to dry while you finish the soup.

Strain the soup through a fine sieve into a clean pan, add the redcurrant jelly, then cook over a medium heat until the redcurrant jelly has melted. Add the cubed breast meat and the remaining mushrooms. Reduce the heat and simmer gently for 8 minutes.

Meanwhile, bring a large pan of water to the boil, reduce the heat to a simmer, add the gnocchi and poach gently for 10 minutes. They will rise to the surface. Remove with a slotted spoon and drain. Add the cream and truffle oil, if using, to the soup, then add the gnocchi. Divide the soup between 4 individual soup bowls and serve immediately.

chilled

The French love radishes, often simply dipped into butter and sprinkled with sea salt. In other countries, radishes often end up as part of a crudités selection or more often added to a bowl of mixed salad leaves. Here's a delicious and unusual way of using them in an interesting summer soup. It can be served hot, too, if you prefer.

radish leaf and spinach soup

15g (½oz/1 tbsp) unsalted butter

2 handfuls of radish leaf tops, coarsely chopped

150g (5½oz) baby spinach leaves

750ml (1¼ pints/3 cups) vegetable stock (see p.22)

4 spring onions, shredded

sea salt and freshly ground black pepper

To garnish

3 tbsp crème fraîche

4 large radishes, thinly sliced

2 tbsp purple shiso cress

The day before, heat the butter in a large pan over a medium heat, add the radish leaf tops and spinach and cook for 2–3 minutes, until wilted.

Pour the stock over, add the spring onions and bring to the boil. Reduce the heat and simmer for 10 minutes.

Transfer to a blender or use a hand-held stick blender to blitz to a smooth purée. Leave to cool, then refrigerate overnight.

To serve, remove from the fridge and season to taste. Divide the soup between 4 individual soup bowls, add a dollop of crème fraîche and garnish with the radish slices and the shiso cress. Serve immediately.

Toasting the garlic and bread in olive oil adds a hint of a warm, nutty flavour to this classic soup, known in Italy as *pappa al pomodoro*. It is simple to prepare, requiring minimal cooking while achieving an impressive result. Ensure that your tomatoes are ripe and sweet. With this in mind, I suggest you wait for summer to make this soup, as that is when tomatoes are sweet, juicy and at their best.

chilled tuscan tomato soup

600g (1lb 5oz) very ripe, sweet and juicy tomatoes

120ml (4fl oz/½ cup) extra virgin olive oil

2 large garlic cloves, thinly sliced

2 slices of crusty white bread, crusts removed and cut into small cubes

2 shallots, finely chopped

150ml (5fl oz/⅔ cup) tomato juice

2 tbsp caster sugar

1 small red chilli, deseeded and finely chopped

2 tbsp balsamic vinegar

juice and grated zest of ½ lemon

sea salt and freshly ground black pepper

To serve

3 tbsp pesto (see p.163)

sesame grissini

The day before, blanch the tomatoes in boiling water, then remove with a slotted spoon to a bowl of iced water. Drain, then peel off the skins. Chop the flesh into small pieces, put in a bowl and set aside.

Heat 3 tbsp of the oil in a frying pan over a medium heat. When the oil is fairly hot, add the garlic and cubes of bread and fry until they are both lightly golden, taking care not to burn them.

Add the fried bread and garlic to the tomatoes, then add the remaining oil and all the remaining ingredients except the salt and pepper. Mix together well. Leave to marinate overnight, covered, in the fridge.

The next day, transfer to a blender and pulse-blitz using the on/off button until the tomatoes are coarsely chopped. Season to taste.

Divide the soup between 4 individual soup bowls and drizzle with the pesto. Serve immediately with the grissini.

I am often asked what are my favourite ingredients. When it comes to herbs, I find coriander and basil both hard to beat. This coriander soup is best made the day before so the coriander has a chance to totally infuse the soup's base stock. Served in small shot glasses or espresso cups, this soup makes a wonderful prelude to a summer dinner party. Other herbs can also be used; basil, parsley, tarragon and chervil, or a mixture of them all, are particularly good.

chilled coriander shots

750ml (1¼ pints/3 cups) vegetable stock (see p.22)

sea salt and freshly ground black pepper

100g (3½oz/3⅓ cups) coriander, leaves and stalks separated

4 egg yolks

75ml (2½fl oz/⅓ cup) double cream

25g (scant 1oz) coriander micro cress or small coriander leaves, to garnish

The day before, bring the stock to the boil in a pan, add a good pinch of salt and the coriander stalks, then reduce the heat and simmer for 15 minutes. Strain through a fine sieve into a bowl and leave to cool.

Put the coriander leaves in a blender. Pour the cooled stock over the leaves, blitz for 2 minutes to a smooth purée, then transfer to a bowl and refrigerate overnight.

The next day, strain the stock again, then put in a pan and gently bring to the boil.

Meanwhile, whisk together the egg yolks and cream in a bowl, then slowly whisk in the chilled coriander liquid.

Return the mixture to the pan, put over a low heat and, stirring continuously, cook until it is almost at boiling point and thickens. Do not let the mixture boil or it will curdle.

Remove from the heat and leave to cool. When cold, refrigerate for 2 hours. Season to taste.

Divide between 4 small chilled shot glasses, garnish with micro cress or small coriander leaves and serve immediately.

THIS PAGE: Guacamole Soup
with Tuna and Prawn Ceviche
(recipe page 204)

OPPOSITE: Chilled Fennel Soup
with Smoked Salmon and Dill
(recipe page 205)

For the best results with this soup, your avocados must be very ripe. I recommend the Haas variety, which I find has the most buttery flavour. This refreshing soup makes a great starter for summer dinner parties.

guacamole soup with tuna and prawn ceviche

3 large ripe avocados (preferably Haas)

1 small onion, grated

1 small red chilli, deseeded and finely chopped

2 tbsp coarsely chopped coriander leaves

juice of 1 lime

200ml (7fl oz/¾ cup) cold white chicken stock (see p.17)

150ml (5fl oz/⅔ cup) double cream

sea salt and freshly ground black pepper

For the ceviche

juice of 2 limes

1 tbsp maple syrup

225g (8oz) fresh best-quality tuna loin, trimmed of sinew and cut into 1cm (½in) cubes

2 tbsp coarsely chopped coriander leaves

2 tomatoes, blanched, peeled, deseeded and cut into 1cm (½in) cubes

150g (5½oz) cooked peeled prawns

½ small red chilli, deseeded and finely chopped

To garnish

10g (¼oz) coriander cress

10g (¼oz) shiso cress

Cut the avocados in half lengthways and remove the stones. Carefully scoop out the flesh into a blender. Add the onion, chilli, coriander and lime juice and blitz to a smooth, silky purée.

Transfer to a large bowl, then stir in the chicken stock and cream and season to taste. Cover with clingfilm, then refrigerate until ready to serve, at least 1 hour.

Meanwhile, make the ceviche. Whisk together the lime juice and maple syrup in a bowl to form a light dressing. Add the remaining ingredients and season to taste.

To serve, place a 5cm (2in) biscuit cutter in the centre of a chilled serving bowl. Add 2 tbsp of the prepared ceviche and gently push it down with the back of the spoon to compress the ceviche slightly in the mould.

Carefully remove the biscuit cutter. Prepare all 4 servings in the same way.

Gently pour the chilled soup into each soup bowl around the moulded ceviche. Garnish with the coriander and shiso cress and serve immediately.

Fennel is one of the least popular vegetables in Britain, which is a great shame. It has a wonderful aniseed flavour that is a great-tasting addition to many dishes. Ask the Italians! This chilled fennel soup is fresh and light and is also delicious served hot, again with the strips of smoked salmon.

chilled fennel soup with smoked salmon and dill

10g (¼oz/2 tsp) unsalted butter

2 leeks, trimmed and shredded

2 heads of fennel, peeled and cut into small pieces

300g (11oz) potatoes, peeled and cut into small pieces

6 star anise

1 litre (1¾ pints/4 cups) vegetable stock (see p.22)

200ml (7fl oz/¾ cup) whole milk

100ml (3½fl oz/scant ½ cup) double or whipping cream

30ml (1fl oz/2 tbsp) anis liqueur (such as Pernod or Ricard)

sea salt and freshly ground black pepper

To garnish

75g (2½oz) good-quality smoked salmon, thinly sliced, then cut into strips

few sprigs of dill

Heat the butter in a large pan over a medium heat, then add the leeks and fennel and cook gently, uncovered, for 8–10 minutes, or until the vegetables have started to soften.

Add the potatoes, star anise, stock and milk. Cook over a medium heat for 25 minutes, or until the vegetables are tender.

Remove the star anise. Transfer to a blender or use a hand-held stick blender to blitz to a smooth purée. Strain through a fine sieve into a large bowl. Leave to cool then refrigerate for up to 4 hours.

When ready to serve, put the cream in a bowl and whip until it forms soft peaks, then whisk the cream briskly into the chilled soup.

Stir in the anis liqueur, season to taste and divide between 4 individual chilled soup bowls.

Top each soup with the strips of smoked salmon and sprigs of dill and serve immediately.

COOK'S SECRET

I was always taught to peel vegetables such as fennel and celery, otherwise they are stringy. Simply peel them using a good swivel peeler.

Some vegetables are as delicious cold as they are hot, and peas are one of them. Look for pods that are bright green in colour and that snap crisply when you bend them. Fresh peas become available in spring, though they are usually tastiest in the summer months. Frozen peas can be substituted if necessary and you can also swap the buttermilk with sour cream. Olive tapenade is easy to make, as you can see, but some good-quality tapenades are sold nowadays in supermarkets and delis.

pea, mint and buttermilk soup with olive toasts

750ml (1¼ pints/3 cups) vegetable stock (see p.22)

2 spring onions, sliced

1 garlic clove, crushed

400g (14oz) fresh peas (podded weight) or 400g (14oz/3½ cups) frozen peas

Small handful of fresh mint leaves, plus a little extra, shredded, to garnish

½ tsp caster sugar

juice of ¼ lemon

100ml (3½fl oz/scant ½ cup) buttermilk

sea salt and freshly ground black pepper

For the tapenade

1 garlic clove, crushed

juice of ½ lemon

2 tbsp capers, rinsed

3 anchovy fillets

150g (5½oz/¾ cup) black olives, pitted

2 tbsp coarsely chopped flat-leaf parsley

4 tbsp extra virgin olive oil

freshly ground black pepper

To serve

2 small bread rolls, each cut into 4 slices and toasted

2 tbsp olive tapenade (see recipe)

The tapenade can be made the day it is needed or it will keep in the fridge, in a sealed container, for 3–4 days. To make, chop all the ingredients and mix together in a bowl. For a less rough version, which I prefer, place all the ingredients in a small blender and blitz until smooth.

The day before you need the soup, put the stock in a large pan and bring to the boil. Add the spring onions, garlic, peas and mint, reduce the heat and simmer for 5 minutes. Do not overcook or the vegetables will lose their fresh flavour.

Transfer to a blender or use a hand-held stick blender. Add the sugar, lemon juice and buttermilk and blitz to a smooth purée. Leave to cool. Transfer to a bowl and refrigerate overnight.

The next day, stir in the extra mint leaves and season to taste.

Divide the soup between 4 individual chilled soup bowls. Serve with the toasts spread with tapenade.

Variation: Chilled Pea, Spring Onion and Crab Soup

Proceed as for the basic soup but top the chilled soup with some cooked white crabmeat and some thinly shredded spring onion instead of the mint leaves.

The last-minute dusting with dried orange powder adds a wonderful burst of flavour to this chilled soup. The powder is easy to make; you will find the recipe for it on page 15, together with many other interesting ideas for its use. This soup is also delicious served hot.

carrot and orange vichyssoise with orange powder

1 tbsp extra virgin olive oil

1 onion, coarsely chopped

1 garlic clove, crushed

1 celery stick, sliced

1 tbsp honey

4 large carrots, cut into chunks

750ml (1¼ pints/3 cups) vegetable stock (see p.22)

juice of 2 oranges

grated zest of 1 orange

100ml (3½fl oz/scant ½ cup) carrot juice (preferably freshly made or bought)

150ml (5fl oz/⅔ cup) double cream

sea salt and freshly ground black pepper

To garnish

1 tsp dried orange powder (see p.15)

2 tbsp snipped chives

Heat the oil in a large pan over a low heat, then add the onion and cook for about 10 minutes, or until softened. Add the garlic, celery, honey and carrots, cover with a lid and cook for 5 minutes more.

Pour the stock over and bring to the boil. Reduce the heat and simmer for 25 minutes, or until the carrots are very tender.

Leave to cool slightly, then transfer to a blender or use a hand-held stick blender to blitz to a smooth paste.

Transfer to a bowl, add the orange juice and zest, the carrot juice and half the cream. Refrigerate for up to 4 hours.

Season to taste, then divide between 4 individual chilled soup bowls. Drizzle with a swirl of the remaining cream, dust each soup with a sprinkling of orange powder, add a few snipped chives and serve.

Variations: Carrot and Ginger Soup Proceed as for the basic soup but omit the orange juice and add a 5cm (2in) piece of peeled and finely chopped root ginger to the carrots in the pan. Omit the dried orange powder but serve with the swirl of double cream.

Carrot Soup with Herb Crème Fraîche Proceed as for the basic carrot soup, omitting the orange juice but finishing the soup with double cream and 1 tbsp crème fraîche, plus 2 tbsp coarsely chopped mixed herbs, such as chervil, basil and tarragon.

This is such a pretty soup to serve on a hot summer's day. It is also extremely refreshing and very delicious. Use thick-set yoghurt for the best results. The recipe for the cucumber granita (shavings of cucumber ice) will make more then you need but you can keep the rest in the freezer for another time.

cucumber and yoghurt soup with cucumber granita

3 medium cucumbers, peeled and deseeded and cubed

sea salt and freshly ground black pepper

2 shallots, coarsely chopped

¼ garlic clove, crushed

3 tbsp lemon juice

20g (¾oz) fresh mint leaves, plus a few extra, to garnish

350ml (12fl oz/1½ cups) natural, thick, Greek-style yoghurt

For the granita

50g (1¾oz/¼ cup) caster sugar

200ml (7fl oz/¾ cup) water

10 mint leaves

1kg (2¼lb) cucumber, peeled and deseeded

1 tbsp lime juice

sea salt

Either the day before or at least 4–5 hours before it is needed, make the granita. Put the sugar and water in a small pan, bring slowly to the boil, then add the mint. Reduce the heat as low as possible and simmer for 3 minutes.

Process the cucumber in a juice extractor or blend in a liquidiser, then strain. Add to the mint syrup. Add the lime juice and a little salt, then strain to remove the mint. Pour the granita into a shallow stainless-steel container and freeze for up to 4 hours or overnight.

For the soup, put the cucumber in a small colander set above a bowl. Sprinkle lightly with a little salt and leave for 30 minutes to draw out the water into the bowl. Set the cucumber water aside.

Place the cucumber in a blender (or use a hand-held stick blender) together with the shallots, garlic, lemon juice and mint. Blitz until smooth.

Add the yoghurt and enough of the cucumber water to obtain a thick creamy soup. Season to taste, then refrigerate for up to 4 hours.

When ready to serve, remove the granita from the freezer. Use the tines of a fork to scrape it into loose, icy shavings.

Divide the soup between 4 individual soup bowls or glasses. Top each with some cucumber granita and serve immediately, garnished with the extra mint leaves.

COOK'S SECRET

When buying cucumbers look for the straight variety. It is said that the straighter the cucumber, the sweeter the flavour!

Daniel is one of the most influential chefs in the USA and has been a consistent culinary leader for many years. His numerous and varied restaurants have an enviable reputation worldwide. He is a true master and all-round perfectionist. I am extremely pleased that Daniel has consented to dedicate his chilled asparagus recipe to my book. Not only is it stunningly beautiful to look at but it tastes wonderful, too.

DANIEL BOULUD'S
chilled asparagus soup with red pepper coulis

750ml (1¼ pints/3 cups) white chicken stock (see p.17)

1 tbsp extra virgin olive oil

2 small leeks, trimmed and thickly sliced

1 potato, peeled, cut in small dice

sea salt and freshly ground white pepper

24 large asparagus spears, (2.5cm/1in of the hard stem end discarded and the rest cut into 1.5cm/⅝in slices)

2 sprigs of flat-leaf parsley, leaves only

For the red pepper coulis

½ tbsp extra virgin olive oil

1 shallot, chopped

2 red peppers, deseeded and coarsely chopped

100ml (3½fl oz/scant ½ cup) white chicken stock (see p.17)

6 drops of Tabasco sauce

Heat the stock in a pan over a medium heat.

Meanwhile, heat the oil in another pan over a medium heat, then add the leeks and sweat for 5–7 minutes, or until soft. Take care not to let the leeks colour. Add the hot stock, the potato and a pinch of salt. Bring to the boil and cook for 6–8 minutes.

Add the asparagus and the parsley leaves and boil for 5–7 minutes over a high heat until tender. Transfer to a blender or use a hand-held stick blender and blitz until smooth.

Season to taste, strain through a fine sieve into a bowl, then place the bowl over ice to cool. When cooled, cover and refrigerate until ready to serve.

Meanwhile, make the red pepper coulis. Heat the oil in a small saucepan over a medium-low heat. Add the shallot and red peppers and sweat for 6–8 minutes until soft.

Add the stock, bring to the boil and cook for 4–5 minutes. Transfer to a blender or use a hand-held stick blender and blitz until smooth.

Add the Tabasco sauce and salt and pepper to taste. Strain through a fine sieve into a bowl, leave to cool, then refrigerate until needed.

To serve, divide the soup between 4 individual chilled soup bowls, then drizzle each soup with the red pepper coulis.

the gazpacho collection

Gazpacho is a chilled soup that is a Spanish national treasure. Here are some of my favourite variations on the theme. All are light and redolent of summer flavours. To enjoy it at its best, gazpacho must be served well chilled. When making the recipes below, I recommend you use a good blender to obtain a nice smooth texture. A hand-held stick blender will give you a chunkier texture that is less authentic.

FROM LEFT: Beetroot Gazpacho with Crab and Mustard Crème Fraîche (recipe page 216); Classic Gazpacho (recipe page 215); Almond, Grape and Cucumber Gazpacho (recipe page 217); Cherry Tomato, Summer Fruit and Hibiscus Gazpacho (recipe page 217); Avocado, Cucumber and Lime Gazpacho (recipe page 216)

1 small red onion, coarsely chopped

450g (1lb) very ripe and juicy tomatoes

200ml (7fl oz/¾ cup) tomato juice

1 red pepper, deseeded and coarsely chopped

1 green pepper, deseeded and coarsely chopped

½ cucumber, peeled and coarsely chopped

2 large garlic cloves, crushed

4 sprigs of basil

1 sprig of oregano

1 tsp caster sugar

100g (3½oz) crusty white bread, crusts removed and cut into small cubes

sea salt and freshly ground black pepper

75ml (2½fl oz/⅓ cup) extra virgin olive oil (preferably Spanish)

2 tbsp sherry vinegar

To garnish

4 hard-boiled quail eggs, cut in half (optional)

8 black olives, pitted and cut into 5mm (¼in) cubes (optional)

5g (1¾oz) Serrano ham, sliced and finely shredded (optional)

The classic gazpacho in all its glory – garnish it as the Spanish do, with all manner of ingredients. I like to serve mine with some hard-boiled quail egg, black olives and shredded Serrano ham, but the choice is yours entirely.

classic gazpacho

The day before, put the onion, tomatoes, tomato juice, red and green peppers, cucumber, garlic, basil, oregano, sugar, bread and salt to taste in a bowl. Mix well, cover with clingfilm and refrigerate overnight to marinate and allow the flavours to blend.

The next day, transfer to a blender and add the oil and vinegar. Blitz until smooth.

Season to taste, then refrigerate again until well chilled.

Divide between the individual chilled soup bowls and top with the garnish of your choice.

400g (14oz) very ripe and juicy tomatoes cut in small pieces

1 small red onion, peeled and coarsely chopped

1 small green pepper, deseeded and coarsely chopped

2 garlic cloves, crushed

2 slices crusty white bread, crusts removed and cut into small cubes

3 tbsp sherry vinegar

2 tbsp raspberry vinegar

2 tbsp caster sugar

4 large roasted beetroots, peeled and coarsely chopped

5 tbsp extra virgin olive oil (preferably Spanish)

To garnish

175g (6oz/¾ cup) freshly flaked white crabmeat

2 tbsp crème fraîche

1 tsp Dijon mustard

1 tbsp coarsely chopped dill, plus extra to garnish

Roasting beetroots really accentuates their natural sweetness and flavour. This beetroot variation is vibrant in colour and has a great sweet-and-sour overtone. I top it with fresh crabmeat lightly bound with a little Dijon mustard crème fraîche with coarsely chopped dill.

beetroot gazpacho with crab and mustard crème fraîche

Put the tomatoes, onion, pepper, garlic and bread in a blender and blitz to a smooth purée.

Put the sherry and raspberry vinegars in a small pan, add the sugar and bring to the boil. Remove from the heat and add to the ingredients in the blender.

Add the beetroot and oil and blitz again to a smooth purée. The flavour should be a balance of sweet and sour. Transfer to a bowl and refrigerate until needed.

To serve, put the crab in another bowl and add the crème fraîche, mustard and dill. Lightly bind together. Divide between 4 individual chilled soup bowls. Top with the crab mixture and garnish with a little dill.

2 ripe avocados, (preferably Haas variety), stones reserved

½ large green pepper, deseeded and coarsely chopped

½ cucumber, peeled and coarsely chopped

1 small green chilli, deseeded and coarsely chopped

juice of 1 lime

100ml (3½fl oz/scant ½ cup) water

2 tbsp white wine vinegar

4 tbsp extra virgin olive oil (preferably Spanish)

good handful of fresh coriander, plus extra to garnish

sea salt and freshly ground black pepper

pinch of ground cumin

To garnish

¼ small cucumber, peeled, deseeded and finely shredded

12 small coriander leaves

10g (¼oz) caviar (optional)

Avocados are one of those ingredients you either love or hate. I can generally take them or leave them but I do enjoy guacamole and that led to this gazpacho soup idea, which is loosely based on that dip. The green colour is stunning. Always ensure you use ripe buttery avocados. Recently, here at The Lanesborough, I topped this gazpacho with an indulgent dollop of caviar. It was a real winner. But you will still enjoy it without, I promise you.

avocado, cucumber and lime gazpacho

Put all the ingredients in a blender and blitz to a smooth purée.

Transfer to a bowl and add the two avocado stones to help stop the gazpacho from going black. Refrigerate, covered, until needed.

Divide between 4 individual chilled soup bowls and garnish with cucumber, coriander and caviar – if you're feeling extravagant!

150ml (5fl oz/²⁄₃ cup) bottled
still water

75g (2½oz/¼ cup plus 2 tbsp)
caster sugar

½ small fresh vanilla pod, split or
½ tsp vanilla extract

100ml (3½fl oz/scant ½ cup)
tomato juice

1 tbsp dried hibiscus flowers

500g (1lb 2oz) ripe summer berries (such as
strawberries, raspberries, blueberries, etc.),
plus extra to garnish

500g (1lb 2oz) very ripe cherry tomatoes
on the vine

8 large fresh mint leaves,
plus extra to garnish (optional)

1 tbsp balsamic vinegar

2 tbsp extra virgin olive oil

Ripe berries such as strawberries and raspberries marry beautifully with other fruits such as tomatoes. Dried hibiscus flowers are one of the new in-vogue flavours for cooking. They have an unusual tangy, herb-like aroma, almost like lemon, and they are high in vitamin C, too. They are also used to flavour drinks – first infused in a liquid then strained. The flower is edible but is hardly used. This gazpacho is a real summery treat that is ideal as a starter.

cherry tomato, summer fruit and hibiscus gazpacho

The day before, put the water, sugar, vanilla pod or extract and tomato juice in a small pan and bring to the boil. Add the hibiscus flowers, cook for 1 minute to form a light syrup, then remove from the heat. Leave to cool, then strain through a fine sieve into a bowl.

Put the berries, tomatoes and mint in another bowl, then pour the hibiscus syrup over. Add the vinegar, mix well, cover and refrigerate overnight.

The next day, transfer to a blender, add the oil and blitz to a smooth purée. Divide between 4 individual chilled soup bowls and garnish with extra berries and mint leaves, if using.

200g (7oz/1¹⁄₃ cups) whole
blanched almonds

350ml (12fl oz/1½ cups) bottled still water

2 garlic cloves, crushed

¼ cucumber, peeled and coarsely chopped

4 slices of crusty white bread,
cut in cubes

150ml (5fl oz/²⁄₃ cup) freshly pressed white grape
juice (preferably Muscat)

2 tbsp sherry vinegar

75ml (2½fl oz/¹⁄₃ cup) extra virgin olive oil
(preferably Spanish)

sea salt and freshly ground black pepper

To garnish

Small bunch of seedless white grapes,
cut in half

2 tbsp toasted flaked almonds

12 small mint leaves (optional)

Whenever I travel to Spain I always try to enjoy this, my favourite, white gazpacho. In fact I prefer it to the classic gazpacho. It is very subtle and nutty, with the sweetness of the grapes adding a burst of flavour that brings the whole dish together wonderfully.

almond, grape and cucumber gazpacho

Put the almonds, water and garlic in a small pan and bring to the boil to take away the raw taste of the garlic. Remove from the heat and leave to cool.

Transfer to a blender, add the remaining ingredients apart from the salt and pepper, and blitz to a smooth purée. Season to taste. If the soup is too thick, add a little more water. Chill until required.

Divide between 4 individual chilled soup bowls and garnish with the halved grapes, flaked almonds and mint, if using.

Dessert soup is an innovative and interesting way to end a special meal. With their delicate sweet taste, fresh fruits play a key role in summer, especially when made into tasty fruit soups. They are light, fresh and cool, and exactly what is needed on a hot summer day. This recipe comes courtesy of my good friend, Pierre Koffmann, a legend of the kitchen for many years. It is both elegant and effortless – a real winner!

PIERRE KOFFMANN'S
soupe de fruits au vin rouge

1 litre (1¾ pints/4 cups) red wine

½ cinnamon stick

10 black peppercorns

150g (5½oz/¾ cup) caster sugar

4 small ripe peaches, skinned

100g (3½oz) cherries, cut in half and stones removed

100g (3½oz/¾ cup) raspberries

100g (3½oz/¾ cup) strawberries

Put the wine, cinnamon, peppercorns and sugar in a pan and bring to the boil. Boil for 3 minutes, then remove from the heat and add the peaches and cherries. Cover the pan with a lid and leave to cool.

When the soup is cold, remove the cinnamon and add the raspberries and strawberries. Leave to marinate for 2 hours, then refrigerate until needed. Divide between individual soup bowls and serve chilled.

COOK'S SECRET

To skin fresh peaches, simply drop them carefully into a pan of boiling water for 1 minute to loosen the skin. Remove with a slotted spoon into a bowl of iced water, then remove and they will be easy to peel.

how to make the perfect

jellied strawberry and tomato consommé with basil sorbet

This is a delicate, light, jellied soup made from the strained essence of fresh strawberries, ripe tomatoes and lemon verbena tea. I like to serve it in chilled martini-style glasses, which makes for a stunning and unusual soup presentation. Accompanied by a delicately fragrant basil sorbet, it really is the perfect summer dessert soup.

200ml (7fl oz/¾ cup) water

100g (3½oz/½ cup) caster sugar

400g (14oz/2¾ cups) very ripe strawberries, hulled and cut into pieces

100g (3½oz) ripe tomatoes

2 tsp raspberry vinegar

100ml (3½fl oz/scant ½ cup) sweet dessert wine

1 tsp lemon verbena tea, tied in a little muslin cloth

5 sheets of gelatine

300g (10oz) fresh summer fruits (such as raspberries, strawberries, blueberries, blackberries, wild strawberries, melon, apricots, nectarines, etc.), cut into small pieces

25g (scant 1oz) small purple or green basil, to garnish

For the basil sorbet

600ml (1 pint/2½ cups) water

300g (10oz/1½ cups) caster sugar

30g (1oz/⅔ cup) basil leaves

juice of 2 large limes

1 To make the soup, bring the water and sugar to the boil in a pan.

2 Add the strawberries, tomatoes, vinegar, wine and muslin-wrapped verbena tea, then reduce the heat and simmer at the lowest heat for 15 minutes. Remove from the heat and leave to cool.

3 Line a small colander with a dampened piece of muslin. Set it over a bowl and carefully strain the cooled fruit mixture through the muslin into the bowl. Push lightly with a spoon to extract as much flavour from the fruit as possible. Transfer the strained juices to a pan and heat until almost boiling.

4 Meanwhile, soak the gelatine in cold water for 2–3 minutes, or until softened. Remove and squeeze to remove any excess water, then stir into the fruit syrup until thoroughly dissolved.

5 Divide the fruits between 4 serving glasses, then gently pour the fruit syrup over to just cover. Refrigerate for 4 hours to set the jelly. To serve, top each glass with a ball of basil sorbet (see below) and garnish with purple or green basil.

To make the basil sorbet

Either the day before or at least 4–5 hours before it is needed, prepare the sorbet. Put the water and sugar in a pan and slowly bring to the boil. Reduce the heat and simmer for 2–3 minutes to form a light syrup.

Add the basil, cook for 1 minute more to infuse the syrup with the basil, then remove from the heat and leave to cool slightly.

Transfer to a blender or use a hand-held stick blender and blitz for 1 minute.

Strain through a fine sieve into a bowl, add the lime juice and leave to cool.

Transfer to an ice-cream machine and churn the sorbet following the manufacturer's instructions.

Transfer to a freezer container, cover and freeze until needed, at least 4 hours. If preferred, make the sorbet in advance and store in the freezer.

The object with this soup is to achieve the right balance of sweet and sour flavours, so you may need to add a little more lime or maple syrup to taste. In Asia, soups like this one are often served hot, too. The lime zest added before serving gives a final burst of flavour.

coconut and vanilla soup with lychees, watermelon and tapioca pearls

200g (7oz/1⅓ cups) pearl tapioca

1 small vanilla pod

100ml (3½fl oz/scant ½ cup) whole milk

200ml (7fl oz/¾ cup) coconut milk

150ml (5fl oz/⅔ cup) double cream

2 stalks of lemongrass, tough outer layers removed and the rest finely chopped

juice and grated zest of 1 lime

maple syrup, to taste

100g (3½oz) Ogen or Charentais melon, peeled and cut into 2cm (¾in) cubes

100g (3½oz) watermelon, peeled and cut into 2cm (¾in) cubes

200ml (7fl oz/¾ cup) canned lychees, drained and cut in half

2 tbsp small Vietnamese mint or regular mint leaves, to garnish (optional)

Put the tapioca in a pan, cover with water and bring to the boil. Reduce the heat and simmer for 15 minutes, or until cooked, stirring regularly.

Drain in a small colander, rinse the tapioca under cold water, then drain again thoroughly. Set aside.

Split the vanilla pod in half lengthways and use a small knife to scrape out the seeds. Transfer the seeds to a blender or use a hand-held stick blender. Add the milk, coconut milk and cream, then blitz until smooth.

Add the lemongrass and lime juice and blitz again until smooth. Strain through a fine sieve into a bowl.

Add maple syrup to taste, then add the cooked tapioca. Mix well and refrigerate, covered, for up to 2 hours.

Divide the melon, watermelon and lychees between 4 individual chilled soup bowls, pour the chilled soup over, scatter over the lime zest and the Vietnamese or regular mint, if using.

COOK'S SECRET

Fresh vanilla is wonderful but is not always readily available. If you can't obtain it, simply replace with ½ tsp good-quality vanilla extract.

This unusual melon soup was a real hit with friends last summer when I served it at a barbecue as a light and thought-provoking starter. I love the combination of goat's cheese and fragrant lavender, but use the lavender sparingly. Wild-flower honey is available from good delis but you could use any honey. Here, I serve the soup in a chilled soup bowl but you could always serve it in the hollowed-out melon shells for a more elegant presentation.

melon and wild honey soup with lavender goat's cheese

4 small cantaloupe melons, deseeded and flesh cut into chunks

1 tbsp wild-flower honey

juice and grated zest of ½ lemon

4 tbsp crème fraîche

sea salt and freshly ground black pepper

To garnish

200g (7oz) firm goat's cheese, loosely crumbled

1 tsp crumbled fresh lavender or ½ tsp dried lavender

Place half the melon flesh in a blender, add the honey, lemon juice and zest, the crème fraîche and seasoning to taste. Blitz to a purée, then refrigerate for up to 2 hours.

Cut the remaining melon flesh into thin slices using a wide swivel peeler or by hand.

Divide between 4 individual chilled soup bowls, then pour the chilled soup over. Carefully transfer to the fridge and refrigerate until needed.

When ready to serve, crumble the goat's cheese into a bowl and season with salt and freshly ground black pepper. Add the crumbled lavender and mix lightly.

Sprinkle the goat's cheese and lavender on top of the soup in each bowl and serve immediately.

index

useful suppliers

You can buy most of the ingredients used in my recipes relatively easily from good supermarkets and specialist delis. Most now carry a wide range of international ingredients for the home cook, while alongside these, many Asian, Middle-Eastern and Caribbean grocers are springing up in areas throughout Britain. Farmers' markets can also be a great place to find specialist produce and, failing all else, the internet is always good, too.

Here are some specialist suppliers for the more unusual produce; the email addresses were correct at the time of publication.

Superb Asian ingredients from **www.japanfoods.co.uk/catalog/index.php?language=en**

Online specialist Asian supermarkets: **www.wingyip.com**

Canned/fresh truffles, truffle juice, truffle oil, caviar, good-quality saffron, dried wild mushrooms and foie gras from **caviar.co.uk**

Smoked butter from The Caithness Smokehouse, **www.caithness-smokehouse.com**

Wild herbs and micro cress, etc. from **www.wattsfarms.co.uk**

author's acknowledgements

I have thoroughly enjoyed writing this book on soup – one of the world's greatest comfort foods. There have been numerous people whose help, encouragement and enthusiasm have been invaluable.

My very grateful thanks go to:

Lara King, for her support and endless typing of my manuscript.

Hilary Mandleberg, for her superb editing and friendship. I know I am in safe hands with her.

Maggie Town, for the beautiful design of the book.

Lisa Linder, for bringing my dishes to life through her excellent photography, and her assistant, Dominika Stanczyk.

Cynthia Inions, for the lovely props she provided for the photography.

Stuart Skues, my executive sous-chef, for his help with the food preparation on the shoots.

And a huge thank you to all my inspirational guest chefs for their friendship and recipe contributions. I am truly honoured to have your recipes in my book. Finally, a huge thank you to Jacqui, Lydia and the rest of Jacqui's dedicated team for their continued support, friendship and belief in my writing.